STUDYING AFRICAN-NATIVE AMERICANS

This book examines the academic study of the African and Native American contact, African cultural change in Native America, as well as the existence of African Americans with Native American ancestry and Native Americans with African ancestry in the Western Hemisphere. Drawing upon the fields of anthropology, history, and sociology that initiated research into these areas, this book attempts to provide understandings of how scholars have studied and continue to understand the experiences of African-Native Americans or individuals of blended – culturally and/or racially – African and Native American ancestry in North, Central, and South America.

It aims to illuminate problems, perspectives, and prospects for interdisciplinary research. The first part is structured to cover the problems – past and present – encountered in investigating the scope of the topic and presents an overview of the most important academic findings. The second part provides both anthropological and interdisciplinary perspectives on the lived experiences of African-Native Americans with both Native Americans and non-Native Americans. And, finally, it sketches out future directions in scholarship.

This book will be of interest to anthropologists, historians, sociologists, and Ethnic Studies and Native American and Indigenous Studies scholars, from undergraduates interested in the topic to graduate students and researchers seeking to interrogate past research or fill explanatory gaps in the literature with new research.

Robert Keith Collins, PhD, a four-field trained anthropologist, is Associate Professor of American Indian Studies at San Francisco State University. He holds a BA in Anthropology, a BA in Native American Studies, and a minor in Ethnic Studies from the University of California at Berkeley. Dr. Collins also holds an MA and a PhD in Anthropology from UCLA. Using a person-centered ethnographic approach, his research explores American Indian cultural changes and African and Native American interactions in North, Central, and South America.

STUDYING AFRICAN-NATIVE AMERICANS

Problems, Perspectives, and Prospects

Edited by Robert Keith Collins

LONDON AND NEW YORK

Cover image: © Kenneth Higgins / EyeEm / Getty Images

First published 2023
by Routledge
4 Park Square, Milton Park, Abingdon, Oxon OX14 4RN

and by Routledge
605 Third Avenue, New York, NY 10158

Routledge is an imprint of the Taylor & Francis Group, an informa business

© 2023 selection and editorial matter, Robert Keith Collins; individual chapters, the contributors

The right of Robert Keith Collins to be identified as the author of the editorial material, and of the authors for their individual chapters, has been asserted in accordance with sections 77 and 78 of the Copyright, Designs and Patents Act 1988.

All rights reserved. No part of this book may be reprinted or reproduced or utilised in any form or by any electronic, mechanical, or other means, now known or hereafter invented, including photocopying and recording, or in any information storage or retrieval system, without permission in writing from the publishers.

Trademark notice: Product or corporate names may be trademarks or registered trademarks, and are used only for identification and explanation without intent to infringe.

British Library Cataloguing-in-Publication Data
A catalogue record for this book is available from the British Library

Library of Congress Cataloging-in-Publication Data
Names: Collins, Robert Keith, author.
Title: Studying African-Native Americans: problems,
perspectives, and prospects / Robert Keith Collins.
Description: Abingdon, Oxon; New York: Routledge, [2023] |
Includes bibliographical references and index.
Identifiers: LCCN 2022042549 (print) | LCCN 2022042550 (ebook) |
ISBN 9781138315235 (hardback) | ISBN 9781138315259 (paperback) |
ISBN 9780429456459 (ebook)
Subjects: LCSH: African Americans—Relations with Indians. |
African Americans—Mixed descent. | Indians of North America—
Ethnic identity. | Indians of North America—Mixed descent.
Classification: LCC E98.R28 C65 2023 (print) |
LCC E98.R28 (ebook) | DDC 305.896/073—dc23/eng/20230125
LC record available at https://lccn.loc.gov/2022042549
LC ebook record available at https://lccn.loc.gov/2022042550

ISBN: 9781138315235 (hbk)
ISBN: 9781138315259 (pbk)
ISBN: 9780429456459 (ebk)

DOI: 10.4324/9780429456459

Typeset in Bembo
by codeMantra

Dedicated to all of my students who have asked why they didn't learn this information until college.

CONTENTS

List of Contributors   ix
Preface   xi

Introduction and Overview   1

PART I
Problems   **11**

1   Problems in the Study of African-Native American Identities   13
    Robert Keith Collins

2   "Detroit Is the Black Man's Land": Internal Colonialism
    and the Problem of Black Indigeneity in Post-Rebellion Detroit   27
    Kyle T. Mays

3   Eugenics as Indian Removal: Sociohistorical Processes and
    the De(con)struction of American Indians in the Southeast   41
    Angela Gonzales, Judy Kertész, and Gabrielle Tayac

PART II
Perspectives   **55**

4   Afro-Native Realities   57
    Sharon P. Holland and Tiya Miles

5 Southern New England Pow-Wows, Race, and Native
   American Identity   83
   Denene De Quintal

PART III
Prospects for Future Research   **99**

6 African and Native American Contact in Mexico, Central,
   and South America: Prospects for Twenty-First Century
   Research   101
   Robert Keith Collins

7 A Final Note   112
   Robert Keith Collins

Index   *120*

CONTRIBUTORS

Robert Keith Collins is a four-field trained anthropologist and associate professor of American Indian Studies at San Francisco State University. Using a person-centered ethnographic approach, his research explores African and Native American interactions in North, Central, and South America. His works include being a co-curator on the Smithsonian's traveling banner exhibit, "IndiVisible: African-Native American Lives in the Americas and African and Native American Contact in the U.S.: Anthropological and Historical Perspectives."

Denene De Quintal is the assistant curator for Native American Art in the Arts of Africa, Oceania, and Indigenous Americas Department at the Detroit Institute of Arts. As the inaugural Andrew W. Mellon post-doctoral curatorial fellow in American Indian Art at the Denver Art Museum, she co-curated the exhibition Eyes On: Julie Buffalohead (2018).

Angela Gonzales is an associate professor and faculty head of Justice and Social Inquiry in the School of Social Transformation at Arizona State University. Her works include being a co-curator on the Smithsonian's traveling banner exhibit, "IndiVisible: African-Native American Lives in the Americas."

Sharon P. Holland is a professor in the American Studies Department at the University of North Carolina Chapel Hill. Her works include being co-editor with Tiya Mile of *Crossing Waters, Crossing Worlds: The African Diaspora in Indian Country*.

Judy Kertész is an assistant professor in the History Department at North Carolina State University. Her works include being a co-curator on the Smithsonian's traveling banner exhibit, "IndiVisible: African-Native American Lives in the Americas."

x Contributors

Kyle T. Mays is an associate professor of African American Studies, American Indian Studies, and History at UCLA. He is a transdisciplinary scholar of urban history and studies, Afro-Indigenous Studies, and contemporary population culture. His works include *An Afro-Indigenous History of the United States*.

Tiya Miles is a professor of History at Harvard University and Radcliffe Alumnae professor at the Radcliff Institute for Advanced Study. Her works include contributions to the Smithsonian's traveling banner exhibit, "IndiVisible: African-Native American Lives in the Americas," and co-editor with Sharon P. Holland of *Crossing Waters, Crossing Worlds: The African Diaspora in Indian Country*, and *All That She Carried: The Journey of Ashley's Sack, a Black Family Keepsake*.

Gabrielle Tayac is an associate professor of History and Art History at George Mason University. Dr. Tayac served on the staff of the Smithsonian National Museum of the American Indian (NMAI) for eighteen years as an educator, historian, and curator. Her works include being a co-curator on the Smithsonian's traveling banner exhibit, "IndiVisible: African-Native American Lives in the Americas," and editor of the volume accompanying the exhibition.

PREFACE

The academic study of the African and Native American contact, African cultural change in Native America, and the existence of African Americans with Native American ancestry and Native Americans with African ancestry in the Western Hemisphere is as old as – if not older than – the American organizations for the fields of anthropology (1902), history (1884), and sociology (1905). It is in these fields and later fields, such as African American Studies, American Indian/Native American Studies, American Studies, Ethnic Studies, and Inter-American Studies, that further the discussion. The guiding premise of this book is that with a subject so vast, no one book can offer analyses comprehensive enough to cover that rich dynamic cultural natures and sources of the phenomena. Therefore, it is important to consider this small book, although guided by Hallowell's anthropological structure for investigating the relationship between culture and experience, an interdisciplinary introduction to these phenomena. The contributing scholars, to all of whom I am deeply grateful for their candor, collegiality, comradery, peer-review, and wisdom, offer perspectives derived from the concern that since initial contacts, particularly those following shortly after the importation of enslaved Africans into the lands that became the United States colony of Virginia in 1619, and renewed attention to these contacts engaged by the Smithsonian's traveling banner exhibit, "IndiVisible: African-Native American Lives in the Americas," the experiences of African descended peoples within Native American cultures and families – both slave and free – remain in need of further academic investigation. This book attempts to provide understandings of how scholars – both academic and professional – have studied and continue to understand the experiences of African-Native Americans or individuals of blended – culturally and/or racially – African and Native American ancestry (Johnson and Smith 1999; Tayac 2009).

To illuminate the significance of this premise, this book is divided into three parts. The first part is structured to cover the problems – past and present – encountered in investigating the scope of the topic and presents an overview of the most important academic findings. The second part provides both anthropological and interdisciplinary perspectives on the lived experiences of African-Native Americans with both Native Americans and non-Native Americans. Like the racism experienced by African Americans in general, African-Native Americans experience racism from Native Americans, White Americans, and ancestral doubt by African Americans that shaped their realities of being American in profound ways. In some cases this racism lends to the eugenic legacy of "black ancestry" being the marker by which one is no longer considered to be of Native American ancestry much like European ancestry. This notion is highly problematic in cases of forced servitude, as will be discussed. These diverse lived experiences and the intersections of culture, kinship, and race the people embody illuminate the importance of prospects for future research.

The cultural, kinship, and racial variations that African-Native Americans embody lend to many expressions of African American and tribal-specific Native American identities. Given the fact that many of the intermarriages and relations that caused African-Native American genesis occurred before federal blood quantum requirements, family and life histories reflective of the dynamics of these interactions, like those in the WPA Slave Narratives, remain frontiers for future analysis of both African Americans that claim Native American ancestry and Native Americans, sold into slavery in states like Texas, that embraced their African ancestry and kinship ties. It is important to note that, despite the racism that surrounds their existence, both populations represent a continuous legacy of respective African and Native American population survival.

It is my sincere hope that this small edited volume will illuminate the research that has occurred, and continues to occur, and lends to understanding the need to study African-Native Americans.

Robert Keith Collins, PhD

INTRODUCTION AND OVERVIEW

When Russell Thornton wrote "Studying Native America: Problems and Prospects" one of his goals was to engage a question that has remained central in the anthropology of the Americas and Native American Studies: "Were peoples and cultures transferred here from Europe and elsewhere transformed by the Native Americans they encountered?" For over a century, this question has received anthropological attention; however, the late twentieth and twenty-first centuries included a revitalization of interest not only by anthropologists, but also scholars in American Indian studies, historians, and sociologists, on an under-researched aspect of this question: the extent to which Africans and their descendants were transformed by contact with Native Americans and vice versa. Although this question is not new, it provides an empirically sound foundation upon which to build an argument for the continued research of African-Native American lived experiences. Nations like the United States, Mexico, and others in Central and South America did not come into maturity merely as a result of Europeans with Native American interactions. It was also interactions that occurred between African and Native Americans and the shared communities, kinship systems, and lifeways that they created together, which lent to the transformation of America occurring in tandem with European and Native American interactions.

Studies of African-Native Americans must continue investigating the realities of cultural changes that occurred between the diversity of Africans and Native Americans. As Thornton reminds us,

> At the least, America was created as a series of frontiers where Europeans, later Euro-Americans, interacted with diverse Native American peoples. Understanding these frontiers is important in understanding Europeans

DOI: 10.4324/9780429456459-1

here, the Euro-Americans they became, and Native Americans after
European arrival, and how each became transformed to form America.
(Thornton 1998: 3)

Does the same not hold true for Africans in America, North, Central, and South, and their descendants? As early as 1891, anthropologist A.F. Chamberlain encouraged us to be mindful of the limitations embedded in the approach and fact that,

> The history of the negro on the continent of America has been studied from various points of view, but in every instance with regard along to his contact with the white race. It must be, therefore, a new, as well as an interesting, inquiry, when we endeavor to ascertain what has been the effect of the contact of the foreign African with the native American stocks.
> *(Chamberlain 1891: 85)*

He also suggested an interdisciplinary approach or extension of "lines of research" was necessary to ensure that investigations were of scientific values (Chamberlain 1891: 85).

It is important to continue examination of this question through an interdisciplinary lens as the fields of African American studies, American Studies, history, Native American studies, and sociology have made – or are currently making – unique contributions to the investigation of African-Native Americans that lend to the expansion of anthropological discourse and potential "unified theories" of African-Native American lived experiences (Gonzales, Kertész, and Tayac 2007; Holland and Miles 2014; Sacks 1989). Anthropological understandings of African-Native Americans have always been informed by the unique lens of other disciplines. During the time of Chamberlain, and at the dawn of academic organization in the United States (i.e., American Historical Association in 1884, American Anthropological Association in 1900, American Sociological Association in 1902, etc.), it was conventional to draw from – and pay homage to – the historical and sociological records on the subject to reveal what scholars already knew. Contemporary scholars are beginning to revisit studies from the various fields on the subject, examine the explanatory gaps, engage in original analyses of racial conflict and the various attitudes that African Americans hold toward Native Americans, Native Americans hold toward African Americans, and examine the implications these hold for the lived experiences of African-Native Americans within Native American communities and beyond. The continuation of this interdisciplinary engagement of the subject seems driven by paradigms and theories within fields on the study of African-Native Americans that suggest such academic research further reveals the dimensions of this third avenue of contact, how it can shed light on the origins of Native American cultural and kinship elements among African descended populations in the Americas, the diverse ethnic and racial variation that individuals of African descent embody, and how blackness has been – and continues to be – used to enable a negation of the African and Native American shared past and present.

The chapters presented in this book reflect the analytical problems, perspectives, and prospects for further academic research on the diversity of this fascinating population and contributes to the ongoing tradition of studying African and Native American interactions in the Americas, questioning tensions between individuals of African, Native American, African-Native American, and European descent, and further highlighting the aspects of lived experiences upon which future prospects in the study of African-Native Americans may be based.

What Is an African-Native American?

Coined during the creation of the Smithsonian's traveling banner exhibit, IndiVisible: African-Native American Lives in the Americas, African-Native American is a term used to describe individuals of culturally and/or racially blended African and status and non-status Native American ancestry. Prior to "IndiVisible" and A.F. Chamberlain's (1891) study, "African and American: The Contact of Negro and Indian," scholars and Indian agents interested in the presence of African individuals within Native Americans communities and individuals of this blended – cultural and/or racial – ancestry began to define African-Native Americans. Rev. Jedidiah Morse's D.D. (1822), "A report to the Secretary of War of the United States, on Indian affairs, comprising a narrative of a tour performed in the summer of 1820," provided evidence of African descended individuals living within Native American communities and nations. Classified according to their "value," African-Native Americans were given a "negro value" if they appeared African American or "Indian value" if they appeared more Native American. In a similar vein, a "white value" was ascribed to those individuals that appeared of blended European ancestry. Although Morse's report was commissioned by the President of the United States to ascertain the state of Native Americans within the current boundaries of the United States, it captured the extent to which those Native American communities, tribes, and nations surveyed contained individuals of African descent.

George Washington Williams' (1883) book, *History of the Negro Race in America from 1619–1800 (volume 1) and 1800–1880 (volume 2)* for example, provided early anthropologists and historians with a clear understanding of the dynamics of intermarriage between Africans and Native Americans in the State of Massachusetts, the common practice for enslaved African men to marry Native American wives, and speculative reasons for why Chief Justice Parker ruled that children born to slave fathers and free mothers were free (Williams 1883: 80). This work, along with John Cromwell's, *The Negro in American History*, seems to have corroborated the research behind Carter G. Woodson's (1920) The Relations of Negroes and Indians in Massachusetts (Cromwell 98–103). Grounded in the first authentic census of the State of Massachusetts in 1765, Woodson notes that,

"The reports on the state of the Indians always disclosed the presence and the influence of Negroes among them" (Woodson 1920: 47). Woodson further noted that social relations were such that tribal affiliations were noted through the mother and while some individuals of blended African and Native American parentage who lived with African Americans occasionally lost community ties and lives as free people of color, others maintained such ties and lived within tribal communities.

Later, anthropologist Melville Herskovits (1928), with the aid of his research assistant Zora Neale Hurston, took a genealogical approach to the subjects of ancestry among African Americans. This simple act of asking African descended people who their kin are was met with great resistance and considered scientifically dubious. Herskovits wrote candidly about the opposition their genealogical approach received,

> The objections to this method are familiar to everyone; indeed, they are stock jokes among Whites, many of whom assert that the sexual looseness of Negro women is such that, the Negro doesn't know who his father is. From this plane the theory goes through various gradations, until it reaches a culmination in the refusal of many of the life insurance companies to insure Negroes on the partial ground that, not knowing their ancestry with reliability, Negroes cannot declare diseases which may possibly be hereditary in their families. The few companies which insure Negroes increase the premium rates for them, again with this reason prominently given. In spite of this argument – and so often is it reiterated that it gains strength even in the minds of the skeptical – I determined to gather genealogies...
> *(Herskovits 1928: 7)*

The findings of this genealogical approach, however, corroborated the oral histories that many African descended individuals maintained about their ancestry. It is important to note that these oral histories were extremely important for African American self-understanding, as the practice of recording all individuals born to individuals of African descent as Negro renders the cultural and racial diversity within an individual's ancestry illusive. For the purposes of this discussion, the findings of Herskovits from a survey of 1551 individuals revealed the following and that Native American ancestry was not a recent phenomenon:

Negro, mixed with Indian	97
More Negro than White, with Indian	106
About the same amount of Negro and White, with Indian	133
More White than Negro, with Indian	75
Total	411

(Herskovits 1928: 9)

As one can see from Herskovits and Hurston's findings, to understand African-Native Americans is to understand African descended individuals that have lived as members of tribal communities voluntarily or by force, families, and nations but also as African Americans. This genealogical approach, like the study of African-Native American in general, enables understanding of the racial variation that the people identify with and embody from common sense understandings of kinship – not merely from how one is recognized or what one appears to be to others. In his dissertation on "Negro-Indian Relationships in the Southeast," Laurence Foster (1978) summarized the problems created by the inconsistencies between cultural identification and racial recognition asserted by African-Native Americans, the practice of Black recognition of African-Native Americans, and misplaced expectations of consistency between how one identifies privately and how one is recognized publicly:

> The general combination of legal status and physical fact has given us a unique situation in the United States. There are a number of persons legally classed as Indian who have far more Negro blood than they have Indian blood. A few of these groups live on reservations legally provided for Indians. A number of these are not even "Indians" from the point of view of cultural anthropology. In other cases, there are Indians who are greatly mixed with Negroes who are Indians in their culture and are legally regarded as Indians. In other instances, large numbers of persons who are mixed with Negro and Indian blood accept the status of Negroes because of the fact that their dominant culture is Negro. Yet, in these instances, these persons often take delight in telling about their Indian strain.
>
> *(Foster 1978: 73–74)*

Foster reminds us that African-Native Americans must navigate between blackness and Native American recognition, often based in blood quantum, despite their culturally based identification practices inherited from family. These "identity struggles," as Wallace and Fogelson emphasized, should encourage scholars to investigate the social phenomena that cause them, rather than lend the illusion that they are inherently individual psychological phenomenon. According to Wallace and Fogelson (1965), "Identities are negotiated through interaction with another person or group." This point holds true; however, it is problematized, as I have found in my own research, when racism shapes the ways in which a child is accepted, rejected, and/or raised (Collins 2006, 2009, 2017, 2021).

The primary objective in studying African-Native Americans can be asserted as follows: to investigate individuals of blended cultural and/or racial African and Native American ancestry and the relationships that have been forged by and between African and Native Americans as universal in the Western Hemisphere. As Foster (1978) reminds us, the importance of this study is to engage how and why,

> A recollection of the slave complex brings to mind the arrival and distribution of the Negro in the New World, which gave rise to the Indians contacts. It was noted that the contacts began in the United States in Colonial Times, and during this period both the Negro and the Indian were slaves.
>
> *(Foster 1978: 73)*

Therefore, the study of African-Native Americans must contain both an investigation of the interactions between the two populations from their origins in slavery to and after freedom. This also means investigating the impacts that Native Americans, as fellow slaves and slaveholders, had on African-Native Americans and African Americans and vice versa (Hallowell 1963; Johnson and Smith 1999; Library of Congress 2021; Littlefield 1980).

An interdisciplinary approach is particularly useful to the study of African-Native Americans because it is through the examination of multiple disciplinary records that the larger picture of African-Native American experiences can be revealed. For scholars exploring the study of African-Native Americans through American Indian studies or Native American and Indigenous studies lenses, liberal arts frameworks have been central to holistic analyses that characterize the fields (Forbes 1993; Hallowell 1963; Thornton 1998: 5). From case studies derived from anthropological, historical, and sociological approaches come analyses ranging from the impact of Native sovereignty on African populations to erasure and racism faced from white Americans. Together this holistic approach has enabled greater understanding of the diversity of lifeways African-Native Americans navigate.

African-Native American, Black Indians, Red Black Peoples, and Freedmen?

One can read throughout the foundational research about many different names for individuals of culturally and/or racially blended African and Native American descent in North, Central, and South America. Prior to the 1960s, the terms Indian-Negroes, Negro-Indians, and Freedmen were used interchangeably over time, to recognize individuals of African descent that lived within sovereign Native American nations as citizens or formerly enslaved populations. The term Mustee was used even earlier to recognize individuals of mixed African and Native American parentage. During the 1970s, the term Red-Blacks coined by Jack Forbes came into usage through his research as a scholar of history and anthropology and later Native American studies. During the 1990s, William Katz brought forward the term Black Indians for public use, which historically referenced individuals of African descent with Native American ancestry. This term was particularly common during the Seminole Wars. While this edited volume used the most recent term, African-Native American, contributors may use the previously discussed terms. The goal of using African-Native Americans is to enable inclusivity and distinctiveness of these shared cultures within this hemisphere.

Overview

This edited volume presents problems, perspectives, and prospects for future research on African-Native Americans and their lived experiences. Each chapter discusses a range of topics from foundational analyses to original academic findings on the subject to encourage both a revisit and advancement of this under-researched phenomenon. Contributing chapter authors have considered the unique elements of the African and African-Native American diaspora within and outside Native America and the enduring relevance of this subject to larger discussion of African cultural change, Native American cultural change, race, and the dynamics of African-Native Americans' being, belonging, and lived experiences. Some scholars bring analyses ground in traditional fields of anthropology, history, or sociology, while others bring innovative perspectives from more contemporary fields like American studies, African American studies, inter-American Studies, and Native American studies. In a similar vein, some scholars are housed in the departments of history and sociology, while others are in the departments of American Indians studies and African American/Africana studies. Collectively the interdisciplinary discourse that comprises this edited volume should encourage readers to draw freely from the various fields, without ignoring the fields in which paradigms and original fieldwork originated.

This edited volume is organized into three parts to provide reflection on foundational ethnographic, political, and social discussions and expand on theoretical issues and explanatory gaps discussed in the literature. The authors in Part I, Gonzalez, Kertész, and Tayac (2007), engage the importance of examining problems in the study of African-Native Americans. Using detailed case studies and reviews of theoretical foundations, the authors explain the nature and sources of cultural, racial, and social problems in the understanding of African-Native Americans and how these shaped being and belonging in African-Native American lives. In Part II, Holland and Miles (2014) and DeQuintal offer perspectives on African-Native Americans in context and the implications they hold for understanding the inconsistencies between what African-Native Americans represent to themselves and others and how this shapes belonging in historical and contemporary lived experiences. Part III provides readers with prospects for inter-American research on the subject of African-Native Americans and a final note that returns to the theme of inconsistencies between identification and recognition that unifies this volume, reviews what this volume accomplished, and concludes how all chapters offer directions for future research into the public and private experiences of being African-Native American.

The chapters in this edited volume while highlighting the problems, perspectives, and prospects for studying African-Native Americans, also suggest new paradigms for examining the breadth, complexities, and dynamics of their lived experiences: (1) the legacies of eugenics and anti-black racism continue to shape African-Native American lived experiences and senses of being and belonging and must continue to be examined historically and contemporarily in the United States and throughout the Western Hemisphere; (2) the extent to which African-Native Americans have internalized these racial attitudes must continue to be examined from what the people say – not just from what is said about them; (3) being African-Native American and belonging among African Americans and Native Americans respectively are not automatic and individuals embody varying cultures and practices.

Chapter 1 examines the anthropological and historical origins of the study of African-Native Americans and the problems that inconsistencies in understanding African-Native American identification and recognition have created over time. In Chapter 2, Mays further engages this problem by examining how African Americans have been cast as "indigenous" in Detroit, Michigan, and how the trope of Indigenous peoples on reservations has overshadowed the cultural creativity individuals used to reassert indigeneity. In Chapter 3, Gonzalez, Kertész, and Tayac's reprint offers readers a reminder of the relationship between social and state recognition policies and practices that define and shape being American Indian, as well as how and why these policies and practices remain in need of ongoing academic attention.

In Chapter 4, Professors Holland and Miles' reprint contributes to a reminder of how and why the inconsistences between African-Native American identification and recognition suggest the need for greater attention to the perspectives of African-Native Americans, if their identities are to be understood beyond the racial ascription practices of public discourse and centered in the intellectual discourse that reveals how scholars have the realities of their existence. Dr. De Quintal's discussion of the relationship between race, Native American identity, and lived experiences at Pow-Wows in Southern New England, in Chapter 5, sheds light on the everyday discourse of anti-black racism and how appearance expectations are experienced, navigated, and negotiated by African-Native Americans. Chapter 6 asserts the importance of understanding the study of African-Native Americans and African and Native American contact as part of the larger process of European and Native American contact and African enslavement and displacement to the Western Hemisphere. Central in this assertion is an examination of the extent of interactions and intermarriage between Africans and Native Americans in Mexico, Central and South America, the interdisciplinary foundations of research on these interactions, and the prospects for future research these foundations offer. The final chapter returns to the goals of this small edited volume, the prospects of future research it provides, and how authors that have contributed to its content, and the lives that have informed their research, reveal how and why African-Native Americans are part of history and a byproduct of African and Native American contacts that have occurred and continue in the present.

Bibliography

Chamberlain, Alexander Francis. 1891. "African and American: The Contact of Negro and Indian," *Science* 17, no. 419 (February 13): 85–90.

Collins, Robert Keith. 2006. "Katimih o Sa Chata Kiyou? (Why Am I Not Choctaw?): Race in the Lived Experiences of Two Black Choctaw Mixed Bloods." In *Crossing Waters, Crossing Worlds: The African Diaspora in Indian Country*, edited by Sharon P. Holland and Tiya Miles, 260–272. Durham, NC: Duke University Press.

———. 2009. "What Is a Black Indian? Misplaced Expectations and Lived Realities." In *IndiVisible: African-Native American Lives in the Americas*, edited by Gabriella Tayac, 183–196. Washington, DC: Smithsonian Books.

———. 2017. *African and Native American Contact in the U.S.: Anthropological and Historical Perspectives*. San Diego, CA: Cognella Press.

———. 2021. "How Did Black Folks Become Indians? What Lived Experiences Say about Belonging, Culture, and Racial Mixture in Native America." In *The Complexities of Race: Identity, Power, and Justice in an Evolving America*, edited by Charmaine Wijeyesinghe, 126–147. New York: NYU Press.

Forbes, Jack D. 1993. *Africans and Native Americans: The Language of Race and the Evolution of Red-Black Peoples*. 2nd ed. Urbana: University of Illinois Press.

Foster, Laurence. 1978. *Negro-Indian Relationships in the Southeast*. 1st AMS ed. New York: AMS Press.

Gonzales, Angela, Judy Kertész, and Gabrielle Tayac. 2007. "Eugenics as Indian Removal: Sociohistorical Processes and the De(con)struction of American Indians in the Southeast." *The Public Historian* 29, no. 3: 53–67.

Hallowell, A. 1963. "American Indians, White and Black: The Phenomenon of Transculturalization." *Current Anthropology* 4, no. 5: 519–531.

Herskovits, Melville Jean. 1928. *The American Negro*. New York, A.A. Knopf.

Holland, Sharon and Tiya Miles. 2014. "Afro-Native Realities." In *The World of Indigenous North America*, edited by Robert Warrior, 550–574. London: Routledge Press.

Johnson, Charles, and Patricia Smith. 1999. *Africans in America: America's Journey through Slavery*. 1st Harvest ed. San Diego, CA: Harcourt Brace.

Library of Congress. "Born in Slavery: Slave Narratives from the Federal Writers' Project, 1936–1938." Accessed June 1, 2021. https://www.loc.gov/collections/slave-narratives-from-the-federal-writers-project-1936-to-1938/about-this-collection/

Littlefield, Daniel F. 1980. *The Chickasaw Freedmen: A People Without a Country*. Westport, CT: Greenwood Press.

Sacks, Karen Brodkin. 1989. "Toward a Unified Theory of Class, Race, and Gender." *American Ethnologist* 16, no. 3: 534–550.

Thornton, Russell. *Studying Native America: Problems and Prospects*. Madison: University of Wisconsin Press, 1998.

Wallace, F.C. and Raymond D. Fogelson. 1965. "The Identity Struggle." In *Intensive Family Therapy: Theoretical and Practical Aspects*, edited by Ivan Boszomenyi-Nagy and James L. Framo, 365–406. New York: Harper and Row.

Williams, George Washington. (1883, reprinted 2014). *History of the Negro Race in America from 1619 to 1880, Volume 2: Negroes as Slaves, as Soldiers, and as Citizens*. New York: Firework Press.

Woodson, Carter G. 1920. "The Relations of Negroes and Indians in Massachusetts." *Journal of Negro History* 5, no. 1 (January): 45–57.

PART I
Problems

1
PROBLEMS IN THE STUDY OF AFRICAN-NATIVE AMERICAN IDENTITIES

Robert Keith Collins

African-Native American recognition, more than identification, has been central in the study of the African cultural change in Native America, particularly among Black anthropologists and scholars of cultural change and race mixture (Chamberlain 1891; Collins 2006, 2009, 2020, 2021b; Forbes 1983; Foster 1976; Hallowell 1963; Sacks 1989; Smedley 2007; Woodson 1920). These two inconsistent practices associated with how humans use identities publicly and privately have created explanatory gaps in the literature and problems for understanding African-Native American identities. This chapter examines the nature and source of these problems, as discernible from the anthropological, historical, and sociological records (Berry 1945; Forbes 1983; Foster 1976; Katz 2012; Porter 1932; Sturm 2002). To contextualize these problems it is important to examine how Africans have been both biological and cultural elements in Native America and how Native Americans have been the same in African America. This argument may seem new; however, it is a revisit of analyses offered by one of the first African American physical anthropologists, W. Montague Cobb (1939: 336). Central in his research on "The Negro as a Biological Element in the American Population," Cobb asserted, "The essential facts about the Negro as a biological element in the American population are common knowledge. He is a hybrid, presenting varying degrees of admixture of African, Indian, and European blood" (Cobb 1939: 336). Cobb also reminded us of the dynamics of African and Native American contact. "In the North and Upper South amalgamation resulted first from contact of Negroes and Indians in servitude and of Negroes escaped to the Indians; later and most important, from intermarriage between free Negroes and reservation Indians" (Cobb 1939: 337).

Consistent with Cobb's analysis, the discussion presented here is grounded in anthropology; however, contrary to Cobb's approach, it will illuminate the

DOI: 10.4324/9780429456459-3

relevance the study of African-Native American identities holds for other fields that emerged after Cobb's analysis, such as Native American studies. The intended goal of this discussion is to examine how research into the inconsistencies between African-Native American identification and recognition can reveal more about African-Native American experiences within the diversity of African American, Native American, and European American cultures from which they descend and have interacted with over time. This chapter continues with a discussion of the problems encountered in researching African-Native American identities. The discussion that follows examines the collective names that have been used to recognize African-Native Americans and the identification problems they created. Lastly, a discussion of primary attributes of African-Native American identities is engaged: African and Native American descendants, former slaves of Native Americans or Indian Freedmen and their descendants, and tribal citizens resulting from intermarriage. Although other physical attributes by appearance, language use, etc. could be discussed, these are central because they are corroborated by academic research, the historical record, and the historical and contemporary lived experiences that informed this chapter.

Problems Researching African-Native American Identities

Since 1891, the literature on African-Native Americans has grown so much that one can hear and read about people recognized as "Red-Black," "Black Indians," and most recently "Africa-Native Americans," but seldom examined is the diversity of the identification practices the people embody (Chamberlain 1891: 85; Csordas 1990; Forbes 1983; Katz 2012; Quinn 2005; Speck 1915). The set of meanings associated with recognition often consists of what individuals represent others racially in public. The common sense meaning in ascription of racial categories is that an individual appears to be of African American and Native American ancestry. In self-ascription of a racial category, the notion communicated publicly – and privately when family identities are consistent with racial categorization – is that an individual views oneself as belonging to the African American and Native American racial categories to enable effective communication of cultural and/or racial ancestry. African-Native American identity in this assertion may contain two components of self-understanding characteristics of identities in the Americas. One, an individual is suppressing cultural or tribal-specific, kinship-based, identities, of which their peers may be unaware, to communicate racial belonging in a manner consistent with social expectations. Two, an individual is communicating one or more racial identities that represent a view of oneself, consistent with the expectations of social peers, because the cultural-specific identities that an individual embodies may no longer be part of self-understanding (Chamberlain 1891; Erikson 1959: 1–21; Quinn 1992: 90; Speck 1915).

Wallace and Fogelson (1965) remind us that the challenges social peers, even family members, raise when an individual asserts an identity that is assumed inconsistent with their own expectations of appearance can create "identity struggles" that reflect negotiations with another person or groups to establish belonging (Wallace and Fogelson 1965: 365–366). Through this practice of making self-understanding synonymous with racial categorization, which Smedley (2007) remind must be understood as a "hereditary social identity" that is based in "...cosmological ordering system that divides the world's peoples into what are thought to be biologically discrete and exclusive groups" (Smedley 2007: 16), the diversity of cultural-specific kinship ties that African-Native Americans embody is undermined and rendered insignificant to the answer to the question, "Who am I?" (Collins 2009, 2021a; Hallowell 1955, 1963; Spivak 1998: 35–37).

The inconsistencies between identification and recognition for African-Native Americans can be seen from slavery to the present. The research conducted by Melville Herskovits (1928), with the aid of his research assistant Zora Neale Hurston, initially highlighted this problem. Both encouraged scholars to remember that the social custom regarding enslaved Africans in the United States and throughout the Western Hemisphere was that,

> Because the Negroes were slaves, the law of the master was paramount; and the masters, as in all slave lands, took the slave women for themselves. But the offspring of a slave was also a slave, and so the mixed-bloods were regarded as "Negroes"...
>
> *(Herskovits 1928: 3)*

Herskovits further reminded scholars interested in researching African-Native Americans that,

> ...there were American Indian peoples throughout the Southeast in the early days, and with these the Negroes mingled to a degree that Whites usually fail to recognize, though to a Negro knowledge of Indian ancestry is a matter of pride.
>
> *(Herskovits 1928: 3)*

Examples like this, of ascriptive racial recognition and the negation of identification of former slaves and their children, can also be seen in the narratives of former slaves of African and Native American parentage obtained by W.P.A. fieldworkers in the 1930s. For example, Ms. Louisa Davis told the following to W.P.A. fieldworker W.W. Dixon in Winnsboro, South Carolina,

> I was born in de Cataba River section. My grandpappy was a full-blood Indian; my pappy a half-Indian; my mother, coal-black woman. Just who I b'long to whem a baby? I'll leave dat for de white folks to tell, but old Marster Jim Lemon buy us all; Pappy, Mammy, and three chillum...
>
> *(Minges 2004: 14)*

The significance of this narrative is that Ms. Davis presents us with a question asked about herself and reflects the inconsistency between identification and recognition in the lives of former slaves: Who did I belong to as a child? It is clear that she remembers her parents and grandfather, their ancestry and parentage; however, identification of self is the prerogative of those who owned her (Spivak 1998: 35–37).

In a similar vein, Ms. Mary Grayson told the following to W.P.A. fieldworker Robert Vinson Lackey in 1937 in Tulsa, Oklahoma:

> I am what we colored people call a "native." That means that I didn't come to the Indian country from somewhere in the Old South, after the War, like so many Negroes did, but I was born here in the old Creek nation, and my master was a Creek Indian. That was eighty-three years ago, so I am told.
>
> *(Minges 2004: 100)*

Another example is the narrative of Mr. Felix Lindsey who explained the following to W.P.A. fieldworker Lottie Major in Wichita Falls, Texas, in 1937:

> I's mo'Injun mix dan I is nigger, but makes no difference. I's a nigger. You all knows how dat is. I's proud of it. I was borned in Rocky Branch, Kentucky, on October 10, 1847. My mother was a half-breed Creek Injun – half-Negro, half-Injun. Her name was Charity. She died 'long 'bout 1853. My father's name was Faithful. He was a full-blood Creek. He was killed in the war 'tween Mexico an' 'Nited States.
>
> *(Minges 2004: 145)*

How does one account for the fact that in one context the identities of these three individuals are determined by their imposed social role as slaves and associated terminology with little to no regard for how they see themselves? This question has not gone away and sheds light on the origins of the myth elements of Native American ancestry among African Americans. These include no Native American blood, ethnic fraudulence, affiliation with a remote ancestor, or a way to explain what many perceive to be non-African features. What these three narratives offer is insight into inconsistent identification and recognition practices that shaped the self-understandings of these former slaves. While in servitude, all three, despite identification with tribal-specific Creek cultural ties like those of Ms. Grayson, or cultural and kinship ties like Mr. Lindsey, who by today's Bureau of Indian Affairs blood quantum standards would be ¾ Creek and only ¼ African, were recognized as African American and the decision for recognition was not based in their own identification practices with cultural and/or kinship ties, but the assumptions of white Americans. Assumptions that they accepted and appropriated as answers to the question, "Who am I?" (Collins 2009, 2020, 2021a; Forbes 1993: 1–5; Hallowell 1963; Library of Congress 2021).

Ms. Grayson's narrative, however, reminds us that, among individuals of African descent, attention was paid to difference between "Native" African Americans and African Americans from southern states. Although these narratives do not represent all slave narratives, they do offer insight into the impacts that the inconsistencies between identification and recognition had on the lives of former slaves and their descendants, and how these oral histories remain frontiers for academic investigation into the inefficient and often negligent recording of the genealogical diversity enslaved Africans and enslaved Native Americans created through shared culture and kinship and their descendants embodied. This phenomenon should not be believed to only hold historical trappings. Throughout fieldwork conducted with the descendants of Africans enslaved by Native Americans during the creation of the Smithsonian's traveling banner exhibit, "IndiVisible: African-Native American Lives in the Americas," respondents revealed the legacy of the inconsistencies between identification and recognition in the present (Tayac 2009).

For example, during an interview used in the exhibit, one respondent asserted the following to me:

MR. REED: ...Because one, being African American, you kind of catch it from the African American community too. There is this whole light skinned – dark skinned thing that, of course, can go all the way back to slavery. There is an issue for the African American community, but for the most part, you're black, so you are accepted. But, you know, every once and a while, there is still that tension. The way I was raised is you know... you are this. This is your background. You're black, you are Euro-American, and you are Native American, but society is going to treat you this way, so be prepared.
ME: How do you cope with this?
MR. REED: I am African American, but I am also Cherokee... At no point in time do I choose, oh I am just Native American. I am just that: A black Cherokee. I also have Euro-American ancestry... but most of all, I am just a human being.

From this narrative, Mr. Reed informs us that despite his understanding of self as African American and Cherokee, his identity is occasionally challenged by non-familial peers and negotiated to establish belonging as an African American and Native American. As a descendant of Cherokee Freedmen or descendant of formerly enslaved African descended individuals among the Cherokee, his narrated experiences suggest an inherent inconsistency between the private identity seldom recognized in the public (Collins 2020, 2021a; Tayac 2009).

What implications do this inconsistency hold for free born African-Native Americans? For individuals the children and descendants of free Africans and African Americans, while this social custom often justified treatment as African American, legal standings – under European and Native sovereignty alike – usually prevented usage as chattel and enabled maintenance of extended tribal-specific identities and kinship ties. Carter G. Woodson (1920) brought attention to this phenomenon in his research, "The Relations of Negroes and Indians in Massachusetts." Examining the historical record, Woodson uncovered many African American families that traced their ancestry back to Algonquin, Wampanoag, and Dartmouth. His research also revealed that, unlike the sparse documentation of enslaved African, enslaved Native American, and enslaved African-Native American kinship ties, in Massachusetts "The reports on the state of Indians always disclosed the presence and the influence of Negroes among them" (Woodson 1920: 47).

The inconsistencies between identification and recognition – what one represents to self and what one represents to others – have become interchangeable components of identity. The dynamics of identity, if not understood within contexts of culture, kinship, and race, can create misunderstandings of heritage and limit understandings of African-Native Americans to race at the expense of culture and kinship. Although this dialectic has evolved over time, the thread that we find between historical and contemporary African-Native American perspectives is that the problem of inconsistency persists (Collins 2006, 2009; Forbes 1990: 1–5; Quinn 1992: 90–92).

Collective Names for African-Native Americans

This history of cultural change among enslaved Igbo, Yoruba, Hausa, Ja, and others and how their descendants became Negro, Black, and then African American is as intriguing as how Cherokee, Choctaw, Creek, Narragansett, Pequot, et al., became Indians and later Native Americans; however, for African-Native Americans, like Native Americans in general, the transformation continues. The ways in which racial categorization lent to the erasure of cultural identities are well documented. For Africans, historians Johnson and Smith (1999) noted this process as a terrible transformation that progressed from kidnapping to indentured servitude to chattel slavery. Within the fields of anthropology and sociology, Russell Thornton has noted the processes of Native American population decline and cultural identity erasure as components of a Native American "holocaust" (Thornton 1987). For African-Native Americans, the forces that caused loss of African and Native American tribal identities are discernible from the historical record and W.P.A. slave narratives; however, these processes remain in need of further analysis.

Two important collective names allude to this process and have subjectively shaped understandings of the population: Mustee and Sambo. Forbes also stressed the importance of researching these terms in relation to the categories of Colored, Negro, and "People of Color" due to their interchangeable usage, especially in the United States (Forbes 1984: 17–18; Zavala 1968: 1–5).

Drawing from anthropological and historical records, and taking the study of Native Americans as the central focus of analysis, Jack Forbes (1983) pioneered a "workable meaning" approach to the terms used to account for "… the interaction of African and American peoples during the first 300 years of European colonialism in the Americas" (Forbes 1983: X). Central in this approach was the goal of using empirical data to avoid misplaced assumptions about the nature of terminology used to describe African-Native Americans. His examination of these data contributed to the development of a body of findings that engaged the source of disagreements among historians on the use of the term "Mustee" (Forbes 1983: 57–58). For Forbes, the source of the disagreement seemed to be the variation in usage of this term. Mustee was commonly used to describe the children born to European and Native American parents; however, it was also used to describe children born to African and Native American parents. Scholars had previously discussed the definition of Mustee as only constituting one population; however, along the Eastern Seaboard in the Carolinas, Georgia, and New York, as well as the English-speaking Caribbean, Forbes found that this term could also be applied to the children of Africans and Native Americans as a way of indicating the Native American parentage or ancestry of an individual (Forbes 1983: 57–60; Webster 1987).

A major part of academic understanding of the term "Mustee" has come from investigations by historians of the breadth and scope of term usage. This includes the ways in which it became interchangeable with the terms "Mestee" in North America and the English-speaking Caribbean colonies; "Mestizo" in Mexico, Central, and South Americans, and Spanish-speaking colonies of the Caribbean; and "Mestis" later Metis in French-speaking colonies. This research examined not only the extent of term usages but also application to people. For example, Winthrop D. Jordan's (1962) analysis revealed that the term Mustee was used in tandem with mulatto, which suggested significant social knowledge of the variations of populations with blended ancestries embodied. The research of Joel Williamson (1980) took a more focused approach and revealed the extent to which the children of Africans and Native Americans were called "Mustees" (Johnston and Jordan 1970: 1–5; Williamson 1980: xii, 39).

For Forbes, however, a different approach consisted of examining how far back this term was in usage, the potential impacts it has on racial social knowledge, and what it revealed about recognition practices in colonial slave holding societies (Forbes 1983, 1993). Forbes examined eighteenth- and nineteenth-century dictionaries for what they reveal about common language usage of the term Mustee. Appearing as early as 1828 in the Noah Webster's dictionary, the term is defined as "a person of mixed breed" and commonly used in the West Indies (Webster 1828). Between 1828 and 1848, term usage seems to shift. John Russell Bartlett's "Dictionary of Americanisms" indicated that a Mustee was a child of a white person and a quadroon (Bartlett 1848, 1860). This term is also suggested to be used in tandem with terms associated with being mulatto. A "mustafina" was the child of a white person and a Mustee and in relation to a Negro, a metif was a mixture of a white person and a "quarteron," particularly in Louisiana. In 1885, Ogilvie's dictionary defines "Mestee" and "Mustee" in nearly the same manner. These were West Indian terms used to describe children of a white person and a quadroon. Subsequent dictionary editions, such as the 1933 Oxford English Dictionary, indicated that the term could be loosely used to indicate a person that was merely half-caste or mixed ancestry (Farmer 1889; Murray, Bradley, Craigie, and Onion 1933; Ogilvie and Annandale 1883).

The evidence, for Forbes it seems, mounted and supported his hypothesis that the term had its origins in recognizing individuals of European and Native American heritage parentage. For those enslaved as a result of war or capture, their enslavement alongside Africans and other Mustee of African descent illuminated another avenue for Native American ancestry among individuals of African descent. Although dictionary definitions were rather consistent, documentation in the historical record, illuminated by Jordan (1962), suggested inconsistencies between dictionary definition and social recognition practices. In early eighteenth century Virginia, for example, Mustee was used to recognize the children of African and Native Americans, as the non-African parentage of African descendants of blended ancestries, slave and free, was more often than not Native American. In South Carolina, Native American slaves were taxed less than other slaves in 1719 to make the distinction between full-blood Native American slaves and African-Native American slave. By this act all Native Americans that were not full-blood would be counted as Negro. In the 1750s, North Carolina policies regarding tithing seemed to make the same distinction (Wood 1974; Wright 1999: 1–5; Webster 1987).

Almon Lauber's (1913) economic study of Indian slavery suggested that under such policies little distinction was made between enslaved Africans and Native Americans or their children (Lauber 1913: 227). The need for such acts and the variation in usage of the term furthered Forbes' hypothesis that there was significant knowledge of the nature of Africans and Native Americans of blended ancestry, as much as there was knowledge of individuals of blended European and Native American ancestry. Forbes' hypothesis is of particular importance to the study of African-Native Americans, since during the latter part of the eighteenth century enslaved Mustees of African descent were recognized as Negro due to their slave status. These inconsistencies between policy and practice remain in need of academic investigation (Forbes 1984: 17–18, 1990; Hurd 1968).

Sambo and Zambo

Through Forbes' research, one can understand the term Sambo, as used in English-speaking colonies, as possibly the most universal term for recognizing individuals of varying degrees of African and Native American parentage in the Western Hemisphere. Zambo by definition was an "African-American hybrid, with no European ancestry" (Forbes 1983: 57–58). Since the early 1700s, colonial societies recognized the children of Africans and Native Americans with this term and distinguishing them from their non-mixed parents. Like Mustee, Sambo was not consistent in usage and distinctions reflected the variations in blended ancestry individual members of colonial societies recognized. For example, throughout the Spanish-speaking Indies, with the exception of Jamaica, in everyday speech a child of a Native American and a "Mulatta" (African and European parentage) was a "Mestize." A child of a Sambo and a Mulatta was considered in certain societies as having the worst identity (Forbes 1983: 57–59; Long 1774: 260–261).

Variations also existed in South America. For example, in Peru, as in all colonial societies, social assumptions regarding ancestry varied and the children of an African and Native American were called "Sambo de Indio," whereas the children of a Native American and a mulatto was distinguished by the term "Sambahigo." As early as 1643, this term as a category of recognition was practiced in New Mexico. Forbes reminds us that, "One partial exception is in Peru where 'Negro' and 'mulatta' and 'negro' and 'india' both yielded 'zambo' or 'sambo de indio' children. Again, however, 'mulato' in Peru implies American ancestry. One also finds such variations as 'dark Zambos' being the children of 'Zambos' and 'Africans,' et cetera" (Forbes 1983: 15 Rosenblat 1954: 167–174). English visitors to Venezuela could be heard referring to African-Native Americans as Zambos as late as 1896. In Mexico, however, lobo, meaning wolf, was the common term used to recognize children of African and Native American parentage. Lobo, also noted in the famous painting of the "castas," seems to have been in use as early as the seventeenth century. Sambo was also used as a racial slur that can be found in the historical record (Forbes 1983:15; 15; Morner 1969: 1–5; Rosenblat 1954: 167–174; Tannenbaum 1992).

Another practice to emerge from the historical record of the British West Indies was the naming of children as Sambo as early as 1690. The British West Indies, particularly Barbados, was of significant interest for Forbes because it was not only the place where a fully conceived notion of slavery was inherited by the United States, it was also a destination where Native Americans from Surinam and North America (e.g., Pequot, Narragansett, etc.) had been enslaved (Dunn 2000: 252, 255; Forbes 1983: 57–62; Johnson and Smith 1999). By the nineteenth century, and with the decline and absorption of Native American populations, African-Native Americans became classified as "colored" or "black." Forbes reminds us that it is important for future research on the nineteenth century to contextualize the terms Sambo and Zambo within the context of these new social recognition practices.

Forbes' analyses and research reflect explorations of a considerable body of literature, created by historians and sociologists, that documented the human diversity created from interactions between Africans and Native Americans within the larger context of blended parentage resulting from African and Native American relationships with Europeans. Like scholars before him, Forbes recognized the caution scholars must exercise in assuming these categories to have been ascribed to individuals uniformly in practice. He asserted that,

> Two other pertinent factors need to be borne in mind: (1) white people often do not actually know the correct ancestry of non-whites and

simply make guesses, often inaccurate; and (2)...Similarly, a ¾ African and ¼ European was called a "Sambo" because he or she resembled a half-American, half-African to whom the designation more correctly applied. More likely, however, all of the "mustees" and "sambos" around the year 1800 actually had some degree of American ancestry; it was simply too difficult to separate with appropriate terms.

(Forbes 1983: 71)

In this usage, as before, American is referring to Native American.

Implications and Conclusion

What implications does this discussion of problems hold for further research on African-Native Americans? The extensive research conduct by Jack Forbes convinced him that the investigation of Black-Indian relations shed light on African descended populations that had "absorbed truly sizeable increments of Native American ancestry" (Forbes 1983: 82–83). Although the majority of this absorption occurred prior to the documentation of the ancestry of enslaved Africans or blood quantum regulations, recognition categories like Mustee and Sambo, according to Forbes, "all of which point to intermixture with Indians – are like artifacts that remain at a campsite after everything else has disappeared or been thoroughly rearranged. These artifacts stand as symbols of what must have gone on before" (Forbes 1983: 82–83).

Renewed interest in African-Native Americans and the relations that shaped their genesis have been presented in Forbes' (1993) "Africans and Native Americans: the Language of Race and the Evolution of Red-Black Peoples." Central in this work is a comprehensive exploration of the development of skin color-based classification systems and how they acknowledged and often overshadowed Native American parentage and ancestry among individuals of African descent. An expansion of this discussion into American studies occurred with Tiya Miles and Sharon P. Holland's (2006) "Crossing Waters, Crossing Worlds: The African Diaspora in Indian Country," and investigation into the lived experiences in the Americas shaped by these systems were engaged as part of Smithsonian's traveling banner exhibit, "IndiVisible: African-Native American Lives in the Americas" and Gabrielle Tayac's (2009) accompanying edited volume.

A major implication of these works is that the study of African-Native Americans and the contact between African and Native American populations the people embody is not arcane. Rather, it is ground in interdisciplinary collaboration and interests with a century-old, empirically sound foundation of academic knowledge upon which to build, as explained in my own research on "African and Native American Contact in the United States: Anthropological and Historical Perspectives." Given the diversity of cultures and populations throughout the Western Hemisphere that were impacted by being classified as "Mustee" or "Sambo," anthropological, historical, sociological, and interdisciplinary questions must continue to be asked if a holistic understanding of this incredible cultural change event in human history is to be understood. Further examination should be possible of how Mustee and Sambo became Negro, then Black, then African American, and how this absorption of Native American ancestry impacted African cultural change in the Western Hemisphere. It will be important to analyze the direct connection between ascribed terminology and populations with diverse kinship ties. The works of Jack Forbes and others that have informed this discussion contain crucial information for understanding African and Native American shared experiences as fellow slaves, during colonization and slavery in the Americas and the shared kinship that resulted. There is a theoretical need for further investigation of the indivisible elements of colonization that both experienced, because both populations have a shared history that suggests race was not the directive force behind their interactions (Collins 2009, 2020; Forbes 1990; Hurd 1968; Sacks 1989; Smedley 2007).

The general discussion of this chapter is that perennial problems and explanatory gaps in the study of African-Native Americans continue to offer prospects for future research. The intended outcome has further revitalized interest in the historical practices used to recognize individuals of blended African and Native American parentage and heritage. Continued examination of the historical record can lend to greater explanations of how racial reductionism is indelibly linked to the patterns by which enslaved and subjugated people have been recognized and how the economic benefits of these categories take precedent over their own identification practices and its documentation (Forbes 1998). A revisit of the complex body of literature created since the late 1800s may further the current explanations of the primary sources that support the empirical foundations of this incredible aspect of contact and cultural change and increase understanding of the inconsistencies between identification and recognition that cause African-Native Americans, Native Americans with African ancestry, and some African Americans to represent an ancestry to themselves that they didn't represent to others, especially those who could not comprehend the "new people" that they embodied.

The goal of the anthropological focus taken and discussed in relationship to other fields is to illuminate the origins of this area of academic interest and the opportunities for interdisciplinary collaboration on unified theoretical approaches that potentially close explanatory gaps in the literature, evident in the foundation laid by scholars like A.F. Chamberlain, Carter G. Woodson, Jack Forbes, and others. It is not sufficient to expect consistency between how African-Native Americans were recognized by colonial societies and slaveholders and how they identified themselves. Such expectations perpetuate the explanatory gaps discussed in the literature. One, the illusion of consistency between social recognition terminology in African-Native American lives and their own identification practices is perpetuated without supporting investigations into the extent to which individuals may have navigated and negotiated socially ascribed racial categories and whether or not these were accepted, rejected, or manipulated by individuals. Without supporting investigations, particularly those that build on Forbes' analyses, it is possible to perpetuate the myth that African-Native Americans were passive recipients of racial categorization.

Two, a fact that is often overlooked, although well documented in the anthropological and historical literature and W.P.A. slave narratives, is that not all colonized and enslaved peoples internalized racial categories as self-understanding (Despite extensive social usage of racial terminology, cultural understandings of self often remain in private usage, particularly within families.) Three, given the incredible cultural, linguistic, and hemispheric diversity that African-Native Americans embodied and continue to represent, and the variation in racial terminology ascribed, expectations of uniform internalization of these categories misrepresent who they are, and the agency exercised in the face of colonization and forced servitude. To understand the problems in the study of African-Native Americans requires a revisit of the inconsistencies between identification and recognition (Collins 2021b; Forbes 1983; Tayac 2009; Thornton 1998).

References

Bartlett, John Russell. 1848. *Dictionary of Americanisms: A Glossary of Words and Phrases, Usually Regarded as Peculiar to the United States.* New York: Bartlett and Welford.

———. 1860. *Dictionary of Americanisms: A Glossary of Words and Phrases Usually Regarded as Peculiar to the United States.* 3rd ed., greatly improved and enl. Boston, MA: Little, Brown.

Berry, Brewton. 1945. "The Mestizos of South Carolina." *The American Journal of Sociology* 51, no. 1: 34–41.

Chamberlain, Alexander Francis. 1891. "African and American: The Contact of Negro and Indian." *Science* 17, no. 419 (February 13): 85–90.

Cobb, W. Montague. 1939. "The Negro as a Biological Element in the American Population." *The Journal of Negro Education* 8, no. 3 (July): 336–348.

Collins, Robert Keith. 2006. "Katimih o Sa Chata Kiyou? (Why Am I Not Choctaw?): Race in the Lived Experiences of Two Black Choctaw Mixed Bloods." In *Crossing Waters, Crossing Worlds: The African Diaspora in Indian Country,* edited by Sharon P. Holland and Tiya Miles, 260–272. Durham, NC: Duke University Press.

———. 2009. "What Is a Black Indian? Misplaced Expectations and Lived Realities." In *IndiVisible: African-Native American Lives in the Americas,* edited by Gabriella Tayac, 183–196. Washington, DC: Smithsonian Books.

———. 2017. *African and Native American Contact in the U.S.: Anthropological and Historical Perspectives.* San Diego, CA: Cognella Press.

———. 2020. "How Africans Met Native Americans During Slavery." *Contexts,* 19, no. 3 (Summer 2020): 16–21.

———. 2021a. "How Did Black Folks Become Indians? What Lived Experiences Say about Belonging, Culture, and Racial Mixture in Native America." In *The Complexities of Race: Identity, Power, and Justice in an Evolving America,* edited by Charmaine Wijeyesinghe, 126–147. New York: NYU Press.

———. 2021b. "Toward an Inter-American Study of African Transculturalization in Native America." In *Colonialism, Coloniality, and Decolonization in the Americas,* edited by Josef Raab and Alexia Schemien, 91–102. Tempe, AZ: Wissenschaftlicher Verlag Trier/Bilingual Press.

Csordas, Thomas J. 1990. "The 1988 Stirling Award Essay: Embodiment as a Paradigm for Anthropology." *Ethos (Berkeley, Calif.)* 18, no. 1: 5.
Dunn, Richard S. 2000. *Sugar and Slaves: The Rise of the Planter Class in the English West Indies, 1624–1713.* Chapel Hill: Published for the Omohundro Institute of Early American History and Culture, Williamsburg, Virginia, by the University of North Carolina Press.
Erikson, Erik H. 1959. *Identity and the Life Cycle: Selected Papers.* New York: International Universities Press.
Farmer, John Stephen. 1889. *Americanisms Old and New: A Dictionary.* London: Thomas Poulter & Sons.
Forbes, Jack D. 1983. "Mustees, Half-Breeds and Zambos in Anglo North America: Aspects of Black-Indian Relations." *American Indian Quarterly* 7, no. 1: 57–83.
———. 1984. "Mulattoes and People of Color in Anglo-North America: Implications for Black -Indian Relations." *Journal of Ethnic Studies* 12, no. 2: 17–61.
———. 1990. "The Manipulation of Race, Caste and Identity: Classifying Afroamericans, Native Americans and Red-Black People." *Journal of Ethnic Studies* 17, no. 4: 1–51.
———. 1993. *Africans and Native Americans: The Language of Race and the Evolution of Red-Black Peoples.* 2nd ed. Urbana: University of Illinois Press.
Foster, Laurence. 1976. *Negro-Indian Relations in the Southeast.* New York: AMS Press. Inc.
Hallowell, A. Irving. 1955. *Culture and Experience.* Philadelphia: University of Pennsylvania Press.
———. 1963. "Papers in Honor of Melville J. Herskovits: American Indians, White and Black: The Phenomenon of Transculturalization," *Current Anthropology* 4, no. 5 (December): 519–531.
Johnson, J. Hugh. 1929. "Documentary Evidence of the Relations of Negroes and Indians." *Journal of Negro History* (XIV): 21–43.
Herskovits, Melville Jean. 1928. *The American Negro.* New York: A.A. Knopf.
Hurd, John C. (John Codman). 1968. *The Law of Freedom and Bondage in the United States.* New York: Negro Universities Press.
Johnson, Charles, and Patricia Smith. 1999. *Africans in America: America's Journey through Slavery.* 1st Harvest ed. San Diego, CA: Harcourt Brace.
Johnston, James Hugo, and Winthrop D. Jordan. 1970. *Race Relations in Virginia & Miscegenation in the South, 1776–1860.* Amherst: University of Massachusetts Press.
Jordan, Winthrop D. 1962. "American Chiaroscuro: The Status and Definition of Mulattoes in the British Colonies." *The William and Mary Quarterly* 19, no. 2: 183–200.
Katz, William. 2012. *Black Indians: A Hidden Heritage.* New York: Atheneum.
Lauber, Almon Wheeler. 1913. *Indian Slavery in Colonial Times within the Present Limits of the United States.* Vol. no. 134. New York: Columbia University.
Library of Congress. "Born in Slavery: Slave Narratives from the Federal Writers' Project, 1936–1938." Accessed June 1, 2021. https://www.loc.gov/collections/slave-narratives-from-the-federal-writers-project-1936-to-1938/about-this-collection/
Long, Edward. 1774. *The History of Jamaica, or, General Survey of the Antient and Modern State of That Island with Reflections on Its Situation, Settlements, Inhabitants, Climate, Products, Commerce, Laws, and Government.* London: Printed for T. Lowndes.
Minges, Patrick. 2004. *Black Indian Slave Narratives.* Winston-Salem, NC: John F. Blair Publisher.
Miles, Tiya, and Sharon Patricia Holland. 2006. *Crossing Waters, Crossing Worlds: The African Diaspora in Indian Country.* Durham, NC: Duke University Press.

Morner, Magnus. *Race Mixture in the History of Latin America*. Boston, MA: Little, Brown, and Company, 1969.

Murray, James A. H., Henry Bradley, William A. Craigie, and C. T. Onions. 1933. *The Oxford English Dictionary: Being a Corrected Re-Issue with an Introduction, Supplement, and Bibliography of a New English Dictionary on Historical Principles*. Edited by James A. H. (James Augustus Henry) Murray, Henry Bradley, William A. (William Alexander) Craigie, and C. T. (Charles Talbut) Onions. Oxford: At the Clarendon Press.

Ogilvie, John, and Charles Annandale. 1883. *The Imperial Dictionary of the English Language: A Complete Encyclopedic Lexicon, Literary, Scientific, and Technological*. Edited by Charles Annandale, M.A. illustrated by above three thousand engravings printed in the text ... London: Blackie & Son; New York: The Century Co.

Porter, Kenneth W. 1932. "Association as Fellow Slaves." *Journal of Negro History* 17, no. 3 (July): 294–297.

Quinn, Naomi. 1992. "The Motivational Force of Self-Understanding: Evidence from Wives Inner Conflicts." In *Human Motives and Cultural Models*, edited by Roy D'Andrade and Claudia Strauss, 90–117. Cambridge: Cambridge University Press.

———. 2005. *Finding Culture in Talk: A Collection of Methods*. New York: Palgrave Macmillan.

Rosenblat, Ángel. 1954. *Poblacion indigena y el mestizaje en America: el Mestizaje y las castas coloniales*. Buenos Aires: Ed. Nova.

Sacks, Karen Brodkin. 1989. "Toward a Unified Theory of Class, Race, and Gender." *American Ethnologist* 16, no. 3: 534–550.

Smedley, Audrey. 2007. *Race in North America: Origin and Evolution of a Worldview*. 3rd ed. Boulder, CO: Westview Press.

Speck, Frank G. 1915. *Nanticoke Community of Delaware*. New York: The Museum of the American Indian, Heye Foundation.

Spivak, Gayatri Chakravorty. 1998. "Race before Racism: The Disappearance of the American." *Boundary 2* 25, no. 2: 35–53.

Sturm, Circe. 2002. *Blood Politics: Race, Culture, and Identity in the Cherokee Nation of Oklahoma*. Berkeley: University of California Press.

Tannenbaum, Frank. 1992. *Slave and Citizen*. Boston, MA: Beacon P.

Tayac, Gabrielle. 2009. *IndiVisible: African-Native American Lives in the Americas*. 1st ed. Washington, DC: Smithsonian Institution's National Museum of the American Indian in association with the National Museum of African American History and Culture and the Smithsonian Institution Traveling Exhibition Service.

Thornton, Russell. 1987. *American Indian Holocaust and Survival: A Population History Since 1492*. 1st ed. Vol. 186. Norman: University of Oklahoma Press.

Wallace, F.C. and Raymond D. Fogelson. 1965. "The Identity Struggle." In *Intensive Family Therapy: Theoretical and Practical Aspects*, edited by Ivan Boszomenyi-Nagy and James L. Framo, 365–406. New York: Harper and Row.

Webster, Noah. 1987. *Noah Webster's First Edition of An American Dictionary of the English Language*, 5th edition. San Francisco, CA: The Foundation.

Williamson, Joel. 1980. *New People: Miscegenation and Mulattoes in the United States*. New York: Free Press.

Wood, Peter H. 1974. *Black Majority; Negroes in Colonial South Carolina from 1670 through the Stono Rebellion*. [1st ed.]. New York: Knopf; [distributed by Random House].

Woodson, Carter G. 1920. "The Relations of Negroes and Indians in Massachusetts." *Journal of Negro History* 5, no. 1 (January): 45–57.

Wright, J. Leitch. 1999. *The Only Land They Knew: American Indians in the Old South*. Lincoln: University of Nebraska Press.

Zavala, Silvio. 1968. *Los esclavos indios en Nueva España*. México: Colegio Nacional.

2

"DETROIT IS THE BLACK MAN'S LAND"

Internal Colonialism and the Problem of Black Indigeneity in Post-Rebellion Detroit

Kyle T. Mays

Introduction

Blackness and indigeneity are central to understanding urban development in postwar Detroit. While this history is typically focused on race relations, in particular Black and white and labor unions and class struggle, Detroit is also a space where various groups have tried to claim ownership in some capacity. Since French settlers arrived in Waawayeyaattanong and planted a flag and changed the name to Detroit, all the way up to the 2013 bankruptcy, the city has been a place rooted in dispossession, enslavement, and racial capitalism. It was a place where Ottawa chief Pontiac, along with allies, fought to end British occupation in North America once and for all in 1763; it was the birthplace of industry and modernity in the twentieth century with the creation of the Ford Motor Company, General Motors, and Chrysler companies. Detroit was also a key place that contributed to the United States' effort during World War II, so much so, in fact, that President Franklin Delano Roosevelt called it the "arsenal of democracy;" it was also the home of a race riot and rebellion in 1943 and 1967, respectively. These histories are well documented. Today, Detroit is known as a Black city, and it remains, per capita, the blackest city in the United States. And yet, the history of blackness in Detroit reveals the complicated relationship between Black Indigeneity and Indigenous erasure. By Black Indigeneity, in the urban context, I mean how Black people use nationalism to assert ownership and lay claims to cities based on their exploited labor, majority population status, and experience dealing with various forms of dispossession, from removal and segregation to the stripping of citizenship rights (Mays, 2021). The focus on this chapter is to demonstrate how discourses of blackness and indigeneity, colonialism, and claims to urban spaces were central to Black radical ideology during the Black freedom struggle of the 1960s and beyond (Rickford, 2017), utilizing

Detroit as a case study. It is an opportunity to think through how dispossession impacts both Black and Indigenous residents in cities. As urban studies scholar Prentiss Dantzler argues, "dispossession involves the explicit taking of both physical land and property and the erasure of symbolic forms of occupation" (Dantzler, 2021, 121). A few scholars have begun to explore these connections within urban studies, but many do not have an explicit focus on history, and certainly don't focus on the relationship between blackness and indigeneity (Dorries et al., 2019).

This chapter asks three questions. First, how can we discuss something like the internal colonization of African Americans without also mentioning settler colonialism? Second, in what ways can Black Indigeneity erase the experiences of urban Indigenous peoples? Finally, and though I don't deal with this question directly but certainly undergirds it, what is the relationship between settler colonialism and racial capitalism within the urban context? This chapter argues that during the Black freedom struggle, some Black radicals used Black Indigeneity as an analytic to make claims to urban spaces. Though I focus on this particular place and time period, these discourses are not new.

Research in Afro-Indigenous Studies has tended to focus on the experiences of the Five Tribes and their enslavement of African peoples, how these relationships existed in the nineteenth century in the southern United States and in Indian Territory (present-day Oklahoma), and contemporary issues within these tribes around citizenship and belonging. In their essay "Afro-Native Realities" in Robert Warrior's edited volume, *The World of Indigenous North America* (2015), Sharon P. Holland and Tiya Miles outline key concepts in the field of Afro-Native studies. "Pain and loss. Slavery and land. These terms map onto and move through one another and are perhaps the primary concepts in Afro-Native studies" (529). Not ending there, they continue to write about the painful reality that Afro-Native people suffer in the context of white supremacy and settler colonialism. While exhaustively outlining the historiography in the field, Afro-Indigenous studies scholarship continues to be stuck within certain parameters. Afro-Indigenous Studies continues to lack critical work outside of the southeastern United States and Indian Territory (present-day Oklahoma), does not engage much outside of the Five Tribes, and continues to focus on the era of U.S. enslavement and the post-Civil War era. Critical to the field, then, is not only an engagement with the problems faced by Afro-Indigenous peoples, but the discourses used to shape public understandings of the links between Black and Native people living in a settler colonial *and* white supremacist society.

At the nexus of Afro-Indigenous studies, urban history, and critical ethnic studies, this essay argues that Black Americans used the discourses of black indigeneity to prop themselves up as "indigenous" to Detroit while at the same time erasing and ignoring an Indigenous presence in the city. This chapter's contribution is a focus on discourses of race and indigeneity in Detroit during the late twentieth century. However, what I do take from the people of African descent on Indigenous land in Indian Territory is that land held multiple meanings in how people constructed their own sense of belonging. As historian Alaina Roberts argues,

> Land claims in Indian Territory came to represent each settler group's ideal of national belonging and citizenship. For African Americans migrating from the United States and Indian freedpeople already in Indian Territory, land held multiple meanings, whether inclusion in the American body politic, an all-Black space freed free from white and Native prejudice, or a place within the Five Tribes. For the Five Tribes, it meant Native nations with few Black or white citizens and the continued insistence on their sovereign right to determine their own citizenship and landownership laws.
> (Roberts, 2021, 73)

The history of African Americans on Indigenous land is complicated, and thus we have to find ways to rethink Black radical versions of land claims that erase Indigenous peoples. There were notable exceptions, including Stokely Carmichael, who, at one moment, argued that Black people needed a land base, but was uncertain if it should happen in the United States. Years later, he argued emphatically, "When you fight for revolution, you must fight for land" but understood "the land in America belongs to the red man. His struggle for his land. It can only be his land" (Carmichael, 1975). As emphatic as Carmichael was, the majority of Black radicals did not fully articulate a vision of land which explicitly made the point that this is Indigenous peoples' land. This essay seeks to unveil a critical understanding of discourse in Afro-Native studies, by combining important conversations in urban history and critical ethnic studies, and how those fields can help expand the field of Afro-Native studies.

Detroit, Black Radicalism, and the Land Question

By the mid-1960s, at the height of the Black Freedom Struggle, things began to change, culminating in the most devastating race rebellion in U.S. history, which occurred in July 1967. The discourses about Post-Rebellion Detroit echo well into the present, and they center on at least three major narratives: (1) Detroit's decline began in the post-rebellion era; and (2) Black people were central to the decline of the city (i.e., unable to govern themselves); (3) Detroit is a place of opportunity, what Quicken Loans owner Dan Gilbert calls "Detroit 2.0." Ignoring the dominant presence of African Americans in the city, Gilbert and others have invited people to come to Detroit and occupy abandoned buildings and space, in order to transform the city; these narratives are reminiscent of nineteenth-century settler logics of moving west and settling in spaces that were unoccupied, devoid of Indigenous people. Therefore, in the contemporary moment, elite white Americans have transformed Black American Detroiters—in their imagination—as an "indigenous" group who neither have control nor have a place in the future of the Motor City. These narratives ignore other factors, including white flight and racist policies such as redlining in the 1940s, as Thomas Sugrue (1996) so eloquently argues. My aim is not to rewrite the history of urban decline in Detroit. However, it is important to note that Europeans have displaced First Nations people of Detroit first, before Black Americans beginning with French colonization in 1701 and has continued through British and U.S. colonization. Although the city has changed, the legacy of dispossession remains, and is deeply imprinted in the city's identity (Kinney, 2018; Mays, 2022).

In the early part of the twentieth century, elite European American men asserted their belonging to Detroit by claiming that they founded the city, and, oftentimes, they used Native histories to construct their own origin story (Mays, 2016). The process of asserting an origins story at the expense of Native belonging to a space is what White Earth Anishinaabe historian Jean O'Brien (2010) calls "firsting and lasting." Detroit has always been an important site for Native people and, unbeknownst to most, remained so well into the twentieth century. European Americans were not the only non-Indigenous group to invoke claims to indigeneity in the twentieth century.

In this essay, I trace the larger ideas of indigeneity as they existed in the Motor City in Post-Rebellion Detroit. I use the term indigeneity to refer to how people—Indigenous and non-Indigenous—construct ideas of belonging and ownership to Detroit. Indigeneity, then, is fundamentally about land and space, and one's relationship to that said land and space. It is both discursive and literal. People connect and understand their identity as it relates to a particular space for various reasons, including because of a sense of loss or a sense of creating belonging in a place that now becomes their home. It also refers to how others identify you to a particular place. In Detroit, Indigeneity is also intimately tied to racialization.

Moving into the postwar era, Black Americans became the dominant group in Detroit. Having come to the Motor City following two World Wars, mostly to Paradise Valley on Detroit's eastside, they became the dominant political group as well. Historian Thomas Sugrue and geographer Joe Darden et al. (1987) have documented the reasons for Detroit's decline and how it became a majority Black city. I will not reiterate that history here. I aim to explain how Black Americans, in a quest to challenge white supremacy and create a sense of belonging in the Motor City, asserted the idea of "Black Indigeneity." I base part of my understanding of "Black Indigeneity" on the work of Shona Jackson (2012).

Jackson's *Creole Indigeneity: Between Myth and Nation in the Caribbean* makes an important contribution to how Blacks in the Caribbean position themselves in relationship to land in the Caribbean, at the expense of Indigenous people. Her framework is useful for also understanding Black ideas in relationship to land, or the city, in the postwar period. Jackson writes,

> *Creole Indigeneity* refers to the practices of belonging and becoming that have provided a new material, symbolic, and discursive relationship to

the land for Blacks, Indo-Guyanese, and Indigenous Peoples. The term captures the unique tensions between settler and native – where native refers to a fixed identity of Indigenous Peoples and the inhabiting of that term by Creoles via their indigenizing and creolization processes – that still operate in Guyana and throughout the Caribbean.

(64)

Black Indigeneity is the idea that Black Americans can construct belonging narratives to a certain place, at the expense of erasing an Indigenous relationship to a particular space. Though responding to the effects of white supremacy, proponents of it used Native histories as a way to imagine a Black future. Black Indigeneity is at once a call to construct belonging to a place which they believe they rightfully earned based upon their labor production; but it is also an idea that reproduced settler colonialism's major goal: Native dispossession and invisibility. Black belonging on Indigenous land remains a contested part of Afro-Indigenous studies. Though instead of thinking of them as outsiders who solely want to replace the Indigenous population, how about we consider this question: when did people of African descent lose their Indigenous identities? If we consider that the enslaved Africans who were kidnapped from their own homelands were Indigenous, how might that help us think through the tension of Black belonging on Indigenous land? Black Studies scholar Tiffany Lethabo King argues that we must think through these relationships in offshore formations (King, 2019).

Black indigeneity is also rooted in the mid-twentieth century's discourse of "colonialism." The term internal colonialism was hotly debated. As Black Studies political economist Ron Bailey wrote, "the principal assertion of our discussion of internal colonialism is that such 'super-exploitation' of black labor is indeed a reality" (Bailey, 46, 1973). Not everyone agreed, but only insofar it did not fit the understanding of colonialism as it existed in the developing world. Black radicals utilized the language of colonialism, making analogies, but did not include settler colonialism, or the experiences of Indigenous people in their analysis, thus creating a tension at the level of ideas.

We might suggest that the election of Detroit's first Black mayor, Coleman A. Young, was the first time in which Black folks became the new "indigenous" community. While Black activism was a strong part of Detroit's history, Young's election made Detroit a Black city¾in political power and, only a few years later, a majority Black space. Indeed, as early as 1970, Detroit's total population was 1,511,482, and the Black population was 660,428¾representing nearly 45 percent of the total population (U.S. Census, 1970). The creation of a Black Detroit was rooted not only in the contested terrains of a Black-White political, social, and economic environment, but deeply embedded within the tensions of indigeneity, that which was caught between settlers (whites) and Indigenous people. Thus, to be Black in Detroit, or rather to have a Black Detroit, suggests also that the shifting nature of indigeneity was no longer in the hands of white Detroit, but now, perhaps paradoxically, within the hands of Black Detroit, an oppressed group, but one who had long waged war within Detroit city politics.[1]

During the height of the social protest movements in the 1960s, Detroit was a hub for Black Nationalism and radicalism. Many groups existed, the religious, Black Nationalist church, The Shrine of the Black Madonna, the Republic of New Afrika, the Dodge Revolutionary Union Movement, even the Black Panther Party had a chapter there (Georgakas & Surkin, 1975; Rahman, 2008). An urban center long associated with the peoples' ability to transform class and racial politics in the United States, Detroit was the place to be, and to seek social change.

Perhaps two of Detroit's most important intellectuals were Grace Lee and Jimmy Boggs. To put it another way, if you were associated with any Black radicalism during that era, you likely engaged with the Boggses. They helped radicalize many people in the Motor City, and contributed significantly to Black radical ideas, which circulated widely. I place Detroit and the idea of indigeneity within Afro-Indigenous studies scholarship that does not rehash familiar narratives, but places primacy on the urban and discourse. These familiar narratives include a focus on the Black people's relationship to the Five Tribes, easily ascribing the label of settlers on African Americans, and ignoring their unique position as enslaved peoples forced to come into a rapidly changing colonial world.

In contemporary discourses about Detroit, popular accounts reference often that the city was built for nearly 2 million people in 1950, which is far above the 700,000 who live there now. In 1950, the Black population was 300,506, and blossomed to 660,428 in twenty years. Black Americans escaping Jim Crow racism in the south and seeking better financial opportunities up north sought refuge in northern and western cities like Chicago, Detroit, and Los Angeles (Grossman, 1989; Self, 2003; Hunt & Ramon, 2010). Many found nothing but poverty, dilapidated housing, and low-paying jobs or no jobs at all. James Boggs was one of those folks who came to Detroit to find work in the north.

Mid-1960s Detroit was a place rapidly changing. But change happened much earlier, beginning in the 1940s. It is important to reiterate that Detroit did not begin to decline right after the race rebellion in July 1967, as the media continues to portray. As Thomas Sugrue (1996) has persuasively argued, racist real estate policies and the construction of suburbs immediately following World War II allowed for middle-class whites and businesses to move out into the suburbs (5, 19). Thus, the rebellion was a reaction to social conditions that had been occurring since the 1940s.

James Boggs was a factory worker who worked in the Chrysler plant for nearly thirty years. He was born on May 27, 1919, in Marion Junction, Alabama, which is twelve miles west of Selma (Ward, 2011, 7). In 1937, at the age of eighteen, Boggs traveled north to Detroit, joining many other Black Americans who had migrated to the city. He then went to his uncle's house on Theodore and Hastings, on Detroit's lower eastside. After settling in and working odd jobs for about two years, he finally found a job at the Chrysler assembly plant on Jefferson Avenue (11). He was also an activist, participating in numerous organizations and engaged with other Black intellectuals throughout the Diaspora, including, for instance, C.L.R. James.

He was a self-described "revolutionist," meaning that he was dedicated to radical humanist change by dealing with social conditions as they actually existed, and constantly learning to deal with new contradictions as they emerge. A brief history of the Boggses and their importance to Detroit's Black radical community helps explain how their ideas circulated, and the significance their words had on others.

Writing was a major part of Boggs' life. He published his first book, *The American Revolution: Pages from a Negro Worker's Notebook*, in 1963. He would continue writing numerous essays, opinion pieces, and pamphlets. One of his most famous pieces, which is the subject of this chapter, "The City Is the Black Man's Land," was originally published in the *Monthly Review* in April 1966. It was later republished in Boggs' *Racism and the Class Struggle: Further Pages from a Black Worker's Notebook*. Boggs wrote this jointly with Grace Lee Boggs, his life partner, who has her own political clout, both as an activist and intellectual within Detroit. This was their first co-published essay. Stephen Ward (2011), who has most recently published an edited book, *Pages from a Black Radical's Notebook: A James Boggs Reader* (2011), interprets this essay as a call for Blacks to take over city politics, and "the black movement" in particular "should focus on establishing urban political power" (22). It was not just a call for community control of politics. As Ward argues, "the Boggses called for black people to claim control over the administrative functions of cities as a whole (as opposed to black sections or communities within cities)" (22).

One of the major arguments the Boggses based their idea of asserting Black ownership of city government was the immigrant narrative. Just as white ethnics of a previous generation, who, when they became a majority, took over city politics, Black Americans, who were then becoming the majority, were "next in line" to take over city politics (Boggs, 2011, 162). They continued, "each previous ethnic grouping achieved first-class citizenship chiefly because its leaders became the cities' leaders"; however, "racism is so deeply imbedded in the American psyche from top to bottom, and from left to right, that it cannot even entertain the idea of black political power in cities" (Ibid.). While the white power structure would hinder Black Americans from taking over city politics, it would only be temporary, and lead to the inevitable: Black people would revolt, even violently. This analysis utilized the language of an immigrant narrative, one in line with the white power structure. It follows the settler logic of occupying space, with the silent narrative of Native people being invisible from the history of city creation and occupation. Thus, the Boggses contributed to the erasure of Native people by virtue of what they did not acknowledge.

The Boggses were asserting a strand of radical Black thought that was tied in with the widely circulating idea of internal colonialism. Their goal, as Ward articulates, was to formulate a "revolutionary theory of black urban struggle that would reorganize not just black communities but American society"

(Ward, 2011, 23). The problems of urban Black America dovetailed those of colonized people in the developing world. For instance, the Boggses argued, "the fundamental problem of the transformation of human activity in advanced America is as deeply rooted as the problem of land reform in countries that have been kept in a state of underdevelopment by colonialism" (165). Utilizing the logic of colonialism, the Boggses were able to place the Black American struggle with the developing world; however, it was not enough to abate the challenges of how colonialism worked abroad versus at home.

Although they were committed to radical social change, they used the history of Indigenous people to erase Indigenous concerns. The Boggses explain the material conditions that exist for the Black community to take over politics in cities. Cities, argued the Boggses, were the central location through which the revolution must occur. They outlined a radical Black political thought for giving the Black community power in cities, especially Detroit:

America has already become the dangerous society. The nation's major cities are

> becoming police states. There are only two roads open to it. *Either* wholesale extermination of the black population through mass massacres or forced mass migrations onto reservations as with the Indians.... *Or* self-government of the major cities by the black majority, mobilized behind leaders and organizations of its own creation and prepared to reorganize the structure of city government and city life from top to bottom.
> *(Boggs & Boggs, 1970, 43)*

On the surface, this presentation is a radical manifesto of Black political takeover of cities, and become a self-determined people. It is a call for Black folks to radically transform the nature of urban politics. Cities are important places to imagine new possibilities for social change. As urban theorist Jane Jacobs (1996) argues, "cities are saturated with possibilities for the destabilization of imperial arrangements" (4). Urban spaces can be places where rapid social transformation occurs, but also serves as spaces that can help "the negotiations of identity and place which arise through diasporic settlements and hybrid cultural forms" (Ibid.). The Boggses were attempting to help shape the theory, which would inform urban political activism. However, there is a certain caution that presents itself in their formulation of reimagining urban space and politics.

For analytical purposes, it is important to re-quote wherein they base their argument. Their argument to take over city politics has two parts. First, cities were the future of radical Black activism. The second part of their argument is subtler, and has been ignored; it was framed as a consequence if Black people do not take over city politics: "There are only two roads open to it. *Either* wholesale extermination of the black population through mass massacres or forced mass migrations onto reservations as with the Indians" (Boggses, 1970, 40). To not take over city politics would not simply be a mistake, but would lead to near extermination and being pushed onto reservations, just like the Indians. Here, the Boggses were using the framework of colonialism, or more precisely the history of Native people, to describe the Black American condition, a prevalent Black radical discourse of the Black Power era.

For instance, Stokely Carmichael (later Kwame Turé) and Charles Hamilton (1967 [1992]) wrote *Black Power: The Politics of Liberation*, a Black Power manifesto of sort. They argued that Black people formed a colony in the United States. "Black people are legal citizens of the United States with, for the most part, the same *legal* rights as other citizens," wrote Carmichael and Hamilton. However, they stood as "colonial subjects in relation to the white society. Thus institutional racism has another name: colonialism" (Carmichael & Hamilton, 1992, 5). They admitted this was an imperfect analogy, but they contended that Black folks had a colonial relationship because of institutional racism. Carmichael would change his analysis much later, strategically including Indigenous peoples in questions of land.

Many Black activists (not all) did not consider actually existing Indigenous people a part of their analysis. And while they could make solidarity with the Third World abroad, they did not understand the nature of settler colonialism in the United States. Indeed, many during this time, and "The City Is the Black Man's Land" in part, utilized the language of internal colonialism to describe the condition of Black Americans in urban spaces. In using Native histories, they mischaracterized Indigenous people as passive, doing little to resist white settler colonial domination.

They ignored Native agency in challenging colonialism before, during, and after the formation of the reservation era. As historian Frederick Hoxie argues, not all Native people resisted militarily. Indeed, many Native activists used "legal reasoning, political pressure, and philosophical arguments to wage a continuous campaign on behalf of Indian autonomy, freedom, and survival" (Hoxie, 2012, 4). We cannot know what the Boggses were aware of Indigenous activism, but given their political astuteness, they surely heard of some activism in Detroit and around the United States. For instance, nationally, the Indians of All Tribes occupied in 1964—briefly—Alcatraz (Johnson, 2008). Also, in 1964, numerous "fish-ins" occurred in the Pacific Northwest, and celebrities like Marlon Brando and Dick Gregory attended, bringing more attention to an important issue to the Puyallup Tribe (Deloria Jr. & Lytle, 1984, 235). By the time "The City Is the Black Man's Land" was published, the Occupation of Alcatraz occurred again, the American Indian Movement officially formed in Minneapolis, Minnesota, in 1968. In Detroit, as my family history suggests, Native people were active in the struggle against racism and oppression in Detroit, including forming a local American Indian Movement chapter and creating alternative cultural and educational institutions for Indigenous people in the Motor City.

The Boggses utilized a history of Native oppression for their own benefit. In other words, they used a form of indigeneity—Indigenous histories within the U.S. settler state—to imagine a Black future free of oppression. Their future ignored Indigenous histories, rendering them invisible. That is, there is no discussion of Indigenous people, who lived in cities like Detroit, and where they would go, or even what their political contribution might be for transforming cities. Thus, Black folks, too, used indigeneity, in this case, the history of Indigenous oppression, for their own political gain, which had the consequence of erasing an actual Indigenous presence in cities.

During the Black Power era, the control of local government and land was a central idea to radical nationalism in the United States. It made sense. As Black Americans aligned themselves within the broader decolonization struggles in the developing world, coupled with the deep, unresolved pain of being the descendants of people who were violently ripped away from their homelands, creating a homeland and being compensated for their exploited labor during and after enslavement was an essential political struggle for some. As Malcolm X articulated in one of his most famous speeches, "Message to the Grassroots," given in Detroit on November 10, 1963, revolution was based upon the struggle for land:

> Look at the American Revolution, in 1776. That revolution was for what? For land.
> Why did they want land? Independence. How was it carried out? Bloodshed. Number one it was based on land¾the basis of independence. And the only way they could get it, was bloodshed.
> *(Malcolm X, 1963)*

Land was central to the Boggses' understanding city transformation and, more broadly, Black liberation. "The fundamental problem of the transformation of human activity in advanced America is as deeply rooted as the problem of land reform in countries which have been kept in a state of underdevelopment by colonialism," argued the Boggses (Boggs & Boggs, 42, 1970). They continued making connections to colonial countries in the Third World and the condition of Black Americans. "Like the colored peoples of the underdeveloped countries," they reasoned, "Afro-Americans have been kept in a state of underemployment" (Ibid).

On May 1, 1965, the Boggses were instrumental in helping to form a national Organization for Black Power. In the founding document of the organization, it stated, "the city is the base we must organize as the factories were organized in the 1930s. We must struggle to control, to govern the cities, as workers struggled to control and govern the factories of the 1930s" (Ward, 2011, 167). The Boggses ended their essay by arguing that at the heart of exploitation was the fact that "the conviction that people of color were not men but subhuman, not self-governing citizens but 'natives'" (170).

Black radicals like the Boggses utilized the language of colonialism and called for Black Americans to take over city politics as the future of the Black revolution. These ideas were based upon widely circulating ideas of decolonization as they were happening in the developing world. However, Black indigeneity, the idea of Black ownership of land and space within a settler state, both ignored Native presences and used Native histories as a prop to construct their own idealistic future.

While I don't want to spend too much time here, other examples include the Republic of New Afrika, which formed in 1968 in Detroit. They called themselves ideologically following the example of Malcolm X who argued that land was central to revolution. They also demanded that the United States give them the five southern states so that they could become a separate nation. An important question that they never seemed to grapple with was how could they make claims to land when, while their ancestors were exploited on that land, it was actually the land of the Five Tribes who were forcefully removed from the area. Now if they wanted to demand land from the Five Tribes because of their enslavement of their ancestors, that would be a different and perhaps legitimate claim to reparations. We will not be able to solve that issue, but it is certainly worth thinking about in future visions of Afro-Indigenous futures.

Conclusion: Black Indigeneity's Possibilities and Potentials

Black Indigeneity has many roots, but I have focused on one particular strand. In the postwar period, radical Black activists have used it as a concept to assert their claims to urban land; they have also used it to construct a Black humanity that was rooted in radical love with the goal of creating a future free of white supremacy. However, it had the major problem of rendering Native people invisible. The rhetoric of Black Detroit continues into the present.

In a December 2015 article in the *Detroit Free Press*, Dennis Black, a 24-year-old activist of Detroit, and one of the founders of the Detroit (local) Black Lives Matter, stated that there is an "urban colonialism that's taken place in the city," and that this struggle is "a continuation of the black radical tradition" (Warikoo, *Detroit Free Press*, December 7, 2015). Black is a part of a broad coalition of organizations including the New Era Detroit, an organization founded on August 17, 2014, and proclaims that they are a part of the genealogy of Marcus Garvey, the Nation of Islam, and the Shrine of the Black Madonna, all Black Nationalist in nature. Organizations like New Era Detroit are rightfully challenging the core of white supremacist state violence that manifests itself in a variety of ways. But at what cost, and how are Native people involved or conceived of in that struggle, given that many are actually indigenous to Detroit and Michigan and Turtle Island more broadly?

There is a lot of potential for the future of Afro-Indigenous studies, and I want to outline a few ways the field might consider going. First, we need to continue to deal with certain analytics, namely thinking more carefully about how Black Americans relate to settler colonialism. Too often, and there are exceptions, Indigenous Studies scholars are too quick to place Black Americans within the settler binary without dealing with the specific problem of enslavement and, subsequently, the problems they face because of white supremacy. Perhaps it is a lack of an actual understanding of history (or training) and acknowledging the persistent trauma of enslavement that Black Americans face. But often scholars will too quickly skirt over the "Black Question" as it relates to settler colonialism, then, perhaps unequivocally, collapse them with European American settlers. Part of the problem, I think, is the anti-Blackness and lack of dealing with the meaning of white privilege that exists within Indigenous studies; that is a conversation for another day that we desperately need to have.

Conversely, Black Studies does not deal nearly enough with settler colonialism; some people deal with it, but it is not even on most scholars' intellectual radar. A part of the reason seems to be that Black Americans, influenced by European American settlers' construction of Native people as invisible (or at least irrelevant to modern political projects). It is also likely that it is a part of the partitioning of ethnic studies; there is also a lack of understanding of the historical relationship between Blacks and Natives, which is too easily reduced to the Five Tribes and enslavement. We need to think more carefully about these historical specificities, and think about how they interact in the twentieth and twenty-first centuries¾not just in the eighteenth and nineteenth centuries.

Another way to reimagine Afro-Native studies is to consider these interactions within urban spaces. When Native people moved to cities in droves in the postwar era, they went to the poorest sections, also where Black Americans lived. What were these interactions like? While historical documentation may be difficult, oral histories provide an avenue to explore these interactions at various moments in the postwar era. There is a lack of urban Indigenous histories, and we certainly know very little of Black-Native relations in cities; that is a project I am currently doing on Detroit. A part of this project is to understand¾systematically¾how Native people have been erased from urban history, and what function that contributes to the larger settler colonial project of Native invisibility.

Finally, one way to assure critical dialogue is to create spaces where we explore the intersections of blackness and indigeneity through culture. Hip Hop is surely one avenue where this happens, and this might serve as a model for unpacking these complex histories and contemporary relations. After all, to quote the homie and Detroit Anishinaabe/Chicanx Hip Hop artist Sacramento Knoxx, can we have a "Black Lives Matter on Turtle Island"? I hope so.

Note

1 In making this claim, I do not mean to suggest that Blacks were an equally oppressive group on par with whites. On the contrary, that would be intellectually inaccurate, even lazy to suggest a thing. However, I do think within cities across America, and in other regions throughout U.S. history, scholars still have a lot of work to do in order to better understand the relationship between blackness and indigeneity, its contradictions, and how we can go forward in understanding these competing and oft-intersecting concepts and people in the twentieth century.

Works Cited

Bailey, Ron. "Economic Aspects of the Black Internal Colony." *The Review of Black Political Economy* 43, no. 3 (1973): 43–72.

Boggs, James. "The City of the Black Man's Land," In *Pages from a Black Radical's Notebook: A James Boggs Reader*, 162–70. Detroit: Wayne State University Press, 2011.

Boggs, James, and Grace Lee Boggs. "The City Is the Black Man's Land." In *Racism and the Class Struggle: Further Pages from a Worker's Notebook*, 39–50. New York: Monthly Review Press, 1970.

Carmichael, Stokely, and Charles Hamilton. *Black Power: The Politics of Liberation*. New York: Vintage Press, 1992.

Carmichael, Stokely. "The Red and the Black." *Akwesasne News*, Winter 1975.

Dantzler, Prentiss A. "The Urban Process under Racial Capitalism: Race, Anti-Blackness, and Capital Accumulation." *Journal of Race, Ethnicity and the City*, June 25, 2021, 1–22. https://doi.org/10.1080/26884674.2021.1934201.

Darden, Joe T., Richard Hill, June Thomas, and Richard Thomas. *Detroit: Race and Uneven Development*. Comparative American Cities. Philadelphia, PA: Temple University Press, 1987.

Deloria, Jr., Vine, and Clifford Lytle. *The Nations Within: The Past and Future of American Indian Sovereignty*. New York: Pantheon Books, 1984.

Dorries, Heather, David Hugill, and Julie Tomiak. "Racial Capitalism and the Production of Settler Colonial Cities." *Geoforum*, August 19, 2019. https://doi.org/10.1016/j.geoforum.2019.07.016.

Dorries, Heather, Robert Henry, David Hugill, Tyler McCreary, and Julie Tomiak, eds. *Settler City Limits: Indigenous Resurgence and Colonial Violence in the Urban Prairie West*. Winnipeg: University of Manitoba Press, 2019.

Georgakas, Dan, and Marvin Surkin. *Detroit: I Do Mind Dying: A Study in Urban Revolution*. New York: St. Martin's Press, 1975.

Grossman, James. *Land of Hope: Chicago, Black Southerners, and the Great Migration*. Chicago, IL: University of Chicago Press, 1989.

Holland, Sharon P., and Tiya Miles. "Afro-Native Realities." In *The World of Indigenous North America*, edited by Robert Warrior, 524–548. New York: Routledge, 2015.

Hoxie, Frederick E. *This Indian Country: American Indian Political Activism and the Place They Made*. New York: Penguin Books, 2012.

Hunt, Darnell, and Ana-Christina Ramón, eds. *Black Los Angeles: American Dreams and Racial Realities*. New York & London: New York University Press, 2010.

Jackson, Shona. *Creole Indigeneity: Between Myth and Nation in the Caribbean*. Minneapolis: University of Minnesota Press, 2012.

Jacobs, Jane. *Edge of Empire: Postcolonialism and the City*. London and New York: Routledge, 1996.

Johnson, Troy. *Red Power and Self-Determination: The American Indian Occupation of Alcatraz*. Lincoln: University of Nebraska Press, 2008.

King, Tiffany Lethabo. *The Black Shoals: Offshore Formations of Black and Native Studies*. Durham, NC: Duke University Press, 2019.

Kinney, Rebecca J. "'America's Great Comeback Story': The White Possessive in Detroit Tourism." *American Quarterly* 70, no. 4 (2018): 777–806. https://doi.org/10.1353/aq.2018.0063.

Mays, Kyle T. "Pontiac's Ghost in the Motor City: Indigeneity and the Discursive Construction of Modern Detroit." *The Middle West Review* 2, no. 2 (Spring 2016): 115–142.

Mays, Kyle T. "A Provocation of the Modes of Black Indigeneity: Culture, Language, Possibilities." *Ethnic Studies Review* 44, no. 2 (September 2021): 41–50.

Mays, Kyle T. *City of Dispossessions: Indigenous Peoples, African Americans, and the Creation of Modern Detroit.* Philadelphia: University of Pennsylvania Press, 2022.

O'Brien, Jean. *Firsting and Lasting: Writing Indians Out of Existence in New England.* Minneapolis: University of Minnesota Press, 2010.

Rahman, Ahmad. "Marching Blind: The Rise and Fall of the Black Panther Party in Detroit." In *Liberated Territory: Untold Local Perspectives on the Black Panther Party*, edited by Yohuru Williams and Jama Lazerow, 181–231. Durham, NC: Duke University Press, 2008.

Rickford, Russell. "'We Can't Grow Food on All This Concrete': The Land Question, Agrarianism, and Black Nationalist Thought in the Late 1960s and 1970s." *Journal of American History* 103, no. 4 (March 2017): 956–79.

Roberts, Alaina E. *I've Been Here All the While: Black Freedom on Native Land.* Philadelphia: University of Pennsylvania Press, 2021.

Self, Robert O. *American Babylon: Race and the Struggle for Postwar Oakland.* Princeton, NJ: Princeton University Press, 2003.

Sugrue, Thomas. *The Origins of the Urban Crisis: Race Inequality in Post-War Detroit.* Princeton, NJ: Princeton University Press, 1996.

U.S. Census 1970, https://www.census.gov/programs-surveys/decennial-census/decade/decennial-publications.1970.html, accessed December 15, 2022.

Ward, Stephen M., ed. "The Making of a Revolutionist." In *Pages from a Black Radical's Notebook: A James Boggs Reader*, 2–34. Detroit, MI: Wayne state University Press, 2011.

Warikoo, Niraj. "A Next Generation of Black Activism Gains Steam." *Detroit Free Press.* December 7, 2015. http://www.freep.com/story/news/local/michigan/detroit/2015/12/07/new-black-civil-rights-groups-detroit-seek-voice/75214942/.

3

EUGENICS AS INDIAN REMOVAL

Sociohistorical Processes and the De(con)struction of American Indians in the Southeast[*]

Angela Gonzales, Judy Kertész, and Gabrielle Tayac

Introduction

The National Museum of the American Indian (NMAI) on the National Mall in Washington, D.C. opened to great acclaim on September 21, 2004.[1] Situated near the U.S. Capitol building, NMAI offers a stark and deliberate contrast to the marble and granite neoclassical buildings of its more conventional neighbors. Among the museum's three permanent exhibitions, *Our Lives: Contemporary Life and Identities* expresses the deeply felt relationship to land, ancestors, community, and the ways Native peoples remember the past. The curators of *Our Lives* posed two critical questions that challenge visitors to reflect on unexamined assumptions about Native identity. Who is Native? Who decides? In this sense, the exhibit provides a convenient jumping-off point to examine how the construction of identity is inseparable from the production of power. Rooted in legitimating public myths of biological determinism and social evolution, these questions persist in contemporary debates regarding American Indian identity, both outside and within Native communities. In this paper we examine how eugenics-informed public policy and social attitudes during the first quarter of the twentieth century served to remove or "erase" from official records Native peoples throughout the Southeast. This kind of documentary erasure does not mean the disappearance of documents, but the use of documents to effect the erasure of Native identity through the manipulation of racialized descriptors as well as the alteration of documents themselves. With its increasing antimiscegenation legislation, arbitrary census enumerations, separate school systems, and bifurcated Southern racial hierarchy where all non-whites belonged to one

---

[*] Note: The piece is a reprint that appears in *The Public Historian*, 2007, Vol. 29 (3), pp. 53–67.

undifferentiated racial group, many of the Southeast's Indians were increasingly constrained by a society that refused to recognize them as anything other than black. As such, Native peoples became the targets of eugenicist policies as exemplified by Virginia's Racial Integrity Act of 1924, which was instated by the state's Chief of the Bureau of Vital Statistics, Walter Plecker. Men like Plecker, who feared White–American Indian intermarriage because they believed that American Indians were already genetically "tainted" by previous intermarriage with blacks, helped promulgate state policies which made it illegal for people to identify officially as American Indians.

One century after The Indian Removal of the antebellum era, Native peoples in the American Southeast provide an important but often overlooked example of how racial policies, this time rooted in eugenics, led to a documentary erasure of Indians as peoples in the twentieth century. We focus on the impact of eugenics-informed policy as it relates to Native peoples as distinct communities rather than American Indians as individuals, since the collective identity of Native peoples is essential to indigenous self-definition and notions of self-determination. The *Our Lives* exhibit, which challenges our understanding of American Indian identity, considers the sociohistorical processes that mediated the de(con)struction of Native peoples in the American Southeast.

Racialization Equals Detribalization

Entering the *Our Lives* exhibit, visitors encounter a public history wherein eugenics-informed policy both reflected and refracted perceptions of Indianness. In the gallery, visitors confront an illuminated wall of photographs. The portraits of Native people cover a broad spectrum of skin color and hair texture – tell-tale markers of identity. These faces defy our expectations of who is Native. A penetrating look from a woman with dreadlocks, an impish grin from a boy with short light hair, a laughing moment caught on camera of a man with straight, long, black hair – stripped of beads, buckskin, and feathers, these images stand in stark contrast to the sepia-tinted photographs made famous by E. S. Curtis in the late nineteenth century. Confronted with faces that do not resonate as "Indian," visitors are challenged to consider their own racialized stereotypes of how Native people are supposed to look.

At the same time, exhibits such as *Our Lives* are part of an increasing movement by Native peoples who have chosen to assert, or "own," as it were, their histories by presenting them in the legitimizing spaces of public institutions such as universities and museums. In so doing, the curators of NMAI, more than half of whom are Native and who represent roughly forty different tribal nations, further challenge non-Native narratives of history by requiring visitors to consider the ways in which a given tribal nation recalls, and has chosen to represent, its own historical experience. The contemporary construction of Native identity, then, invariably constitutes the ways in which tribal histories were experienced, and the ways in which tribal peoples have chosen to remember and interpret them – a phenomenon that may not readily translate into constructions of identity that are biologically driven.

The construction of a physical identity steeped in biological race-based notions of human types was a late eighteenth-, early nineteenth-century European development. With its advancement, physical and social scientists made the politically useful declaration of an irrefutable biological basis for race. This "scientific" development concretely defined the so-called "races" as distinct genetic population categories whose identity could be objectively determined and quantified by their blood.[2] The idea of "racial blood" was aided by the work of the father of eugenics, Francis Galton, who developed a theory of fractional inheritance whereby every person was believed to receive one-half of their hereditary endowment from each parent, one-fourth from each grandparent, and so on.[3]

Throughout the United States, and especially in the South, legislated race codes that predate the work of Galton already quantified identity based upon a percentage of blood. The practice of hypodescent for determining the identity of persons of mixed ancestry was imbricated in policies that classified and assigned identity based on the race of a person's more socially subordinate parent. For example, in 1866, the State of Virginia declared that "every person having one-fourth or more Negro blood shall be deemed a colored person, and every person not a colored person having one-fourth or more Indian blood shall be deemed an Indian."[4] The application of hypodescent later diverged to define as "Black" a person with any known black ancestry and as "American Indian" a person with some minimum amount of Indian ancestry.[5] This systematic categorization of race with its rules governing identity served to maintain not only white power and authority, but also as justification for black slavery and the dispossession of land from Native peoples. The amount of "blood" required to be Indian (one-quarter) or black (one drop) reflected the difference in white attitudes toward Indians and blacks. This racialization of identity, based on the ideology of biological inheritance and racial hierarchy, was a powerful and pervasive force that facilitated the dispossession and displacement of Native identity in the Southeast. A real or perceived black–Native admixture could and historically did cancel out self-ascribed tribal identities for individuals and entire communities.

Throughout the nineteenth century, and most markedly after the Indian removals of the 1830s, individuals belonging to many of the Southeast's tribal nations were often reclassified. At the same time, their collective tribal identity was disbanded once they were redefined in racialized rather than legal terms as entities with a government-to-government relationship. Many of the Southeast's tribal peoples, then, were individually defined by an externally imposed racial category that nullified claims to a collective identity circumscribed by racialized restrictions that were increasingly codified.

Fractured Genealogies

As visitors to the *Our Lives* exhibit make their way around the illuminated wall of photographic images, they are confronted with documents and images that further challenge their assumptions about what constitutes Native identity. The exhibit asks: Is my identity a number, an artifact, a piece of paper, a scientific chart, in my blood? Is my identity how I look? Does my identity come from the government?[6] These and similar questions informed the context for the eugenics-oriented policies that affected Native peoples of the Southeast in the first half of the twentieth century. To understand the deeply embedded and entangled roots of eugenics policy in the Southeast, one need only recall the social and economic upheaval of the post–Civil War years to make appreciable the anxieties of a profoundly troubled white population invested in keeping separate other races that had just been declared equal.

The years following the Civil War culminating in the Progressive era from 1880 to 1920 witnessed rapid economic, political, and social change. In the aftermath of war, the industrialized North recovered rapidly, unlike the beleaguered rural South, which was struggling through its own societal and economic reconstruction. The development of eugenics in the American South was in part an outgrowth of the anxieties that came with change that in turn increased the need for progressive reform. Progressivists of the late nineteenth and early twentieth century sought to apply cures to a society disrupted by the antisocial behavior of individuals or whole groups by combining the expression of science with humanism.[7] Eugenics was first and foremost an ideology rooted in science. Even though eugenics has its origins in Great Britain, biologists and zoologists in major research universities in the United States developed many of its precepts by conducting studies in the isolated rural communities, or "so called pockets of degeneracy" of the north and southeast.[8] A closer consideration of the history of eugenics also illustrates the ways in which universities and state and federal governments found themselves intervening in questions of Native identity. In such cases, notions of blood and descent were bound up with perceptions of authenticity and the defective biology that "tainted" certain individuals and the communities to which they belonged.

Two methodological approaches used by university researchers during the first quarter of the twentieth century to assess and categorize racial and hereditary health were pedigree analysis and statistical correlations. Researchers believed that the study of human traits could eventually unravel the complexities of human heredity and that such knowledge could be applied to improve a society afflicted by social, reproductive, and economic health problems.[9] Increasingly ill at ease with the effects of immigration, rural decline, poverty, criminality, and their perceived connections to "feeblemindedness," Northern progressives, many of them descendants of "old colonial stocks," embraced scientific studies and surveys first pioneered by geneticists such as Richard L. Dugdale. Dugdale furnished some of the basis for the new scientific and social movement of eugenics by combing the records of county courts, jails, and poor houses in order to chart seven generations of one family, the Jukes, and their "genealogy of degeneracy."[10]

In the intervening four decades, eugenicists such as Henry H. Goddard and Harvard zoologist Charles Davenport wrote representative works on "inbred" rural populations, "feeblemindedness," and criminality that decontextualized the historical experience of families caught in the cycle of discrimination, poverty, and limited access to resources.[11] Their studies reinforced the notion of the immutability of inheritable traits, compelling progressive Northerners to implement legal restrictions to limit immigration while assessing the merits of involuntary sterilization and legislative restrictions on marriage.[12] In 1924, the federal government passed the Johnson-Reed Act, which restricted immigration from the Mediterranean and Eastern Europe, while on the state level, eugenicists also effectively lobbied for eugenic sterilization legislation.[13]

The American Southeast was slower to consider scientifically based technologies for reducing instances of family, and by extension, ethnic and racial degeneracy.[14] Although laws forbidding marriages to those who were underage or "feebleminded" were already in place throughout the country, only the South maintained strict antimiscegenation statutes which, given the conclusions drawn in subsequent eugenics studies, had proven entirely ineffective in stemming the tide of racial degeneration. Even so, in 1919, 1929, 1933, and 1935, North Carolina passed sterilization laws that were later deemed unconstitutional.[15] Virginia did the same in 1924. However, according to the records of the Eugenics Board of North Carolina, from 1935 until 1954, not one American Indian was sterilized by the state.[16] The reasons for this are readily appreciable. Sterilizations were largely performed in state-run health service facilities that restricted access to whites. Given this access, "degenerate" white individuals bore the initial brunt of eugenics inspired sterilization. This is not to argue that sterilization of American Indians in significantly larger numbers did not take place. For example, in the 1970s, documented sterilizations performed by the Indian Health Service (IHS), a federal agency that serviced American Indians, indicate widespread sterilization abuse due to coercion, improper consent forms, and by failing to provide appropriate waiting periods. In 1975 alone, IHS sterilized roughly 25,000 American Indian women. Therefore, sterilization as a historical experience in Indian Country was a more recent phenomenon federal in scope that, for the most part, affected Native populations west of the Mississippi.[17]

Access to state-run health services for African Americans and American Indians began to change in 1954 with the passage of *Brown v. Board of Education* – legislation that required schools to desegregate, and later paved the way for other public facilities to do the same.[18] The sterilization of African Americans in North Carolina increased steadily after 1954, surpassing the number of sterilizations of white Americans within four years. From 1954 until 1968, North Carolina sterilized 44 Indians.[19] The manner in which eugenics affected American Indians of the Southeast during the years between the two world wars did not manifest itself medically through sterilization.

Southeastern eugenicists instead sought to remedy social blights and alleviate white anxieties administratively. Continuing Richard Dugdale's genealogical study of the Jukes family, Arthur H. Estabrook conducted further genealogical sleuthing in the Southeast with the assistance of Ivan E. McDougle and eventually published *Mongrel Virginians*.[20] Estabrook and McDougle's "mongrels," were the Monacan Indians of Virginia's Amherst county, "described variously as 'low down' yellow Negroes, as Indians, as 'mixed.'"[21] Their study, following on the heels of Virginia's passage of the Racial Integrity Act of 1924, was well received by Walter Ashby Plecker, Virginia's registrar of the Bureau of Vital Statistics.[22] Bureau officials had noted a marked drop in the state's mulatto population on the 1920 census – the last year that the census included mulatto as a racial category. Some suspected that passing might be the reason. Using the weight of his office, Plecker, who ran the Bureau from its inception in 1912 until 1946, enjoined town clerks throughout Virginia to classify anyone claiming to be Indian as black. With its erroneous focus on inferior and superior human types based on heredity interpreted frequently as race, the translation of eugenics from ideology to policy proved to be an appealing strategy for Plecker. The Racial Integrity Act barred racial intermarriage and divided Virginia's population into firmly immutable categories. Whites were defined as those people having "no trace whatever of any blood other than Caucasian." However, since several prominent elite Virginians traced their ancestry to Pocahontas, Plecker was forced to concede that whites having one-sixteenth or less American Indian blood could still be legally classified as white.[23]

Reorganizing Native Peoples though Racial Diagnostics

Following a forty-year period of concentrated effort to assimilate American Indians, Congress passed the Indian Reorganization Act (IRA) in 1934 which, among other things, stopped the allotment of tribal lands, provided money for reservation economic development, encouraged tribes to adopt a constitutional form of government, and utilized criteria for quantifying Native identity through "blood quantum."[24] Determining an individual's blood quantum, however, required a benchmark. Shortly after passage of the Indian Reorganization Act in 1934, federal enumerators began canvassing Indian lands, counting Indian households, recording the number of adults and children and the presumed blood quantum of each. Although the IRA seemed to provide precise criteria for determining racial boundaries, it was not so easy to implement these definitions in practice. Individuals were generally not able to develop genealogical proofs of their "blood quantum" and decisions regarding an individual's degree of Indian blood relied as much on the subjective judgments of enumerators and the presumed racial characteristics associated with skin color, facial features, hair texture, and body odor. Although "blood quantum" appeared objective when written into statute, a lay constructivist conception is what was actually used in practice. Prior to the IRA's passage, federal statutes rarely defined the terms "tribe" or "Indian." Although tribes had long been recognized vis-à-vis treaties and executive orders, "federal recognition" as a conceptual category was not formally articulated until passage of the IRA:

> The term "Indian" as used in this Act shall include all persons of Indian descent who are members *of any recognized Indian tribe now under Federal jurisdiction*, and all persons who are descendants of such members who were, on June 1, 1934, residing within the present boundaries of any Indian reservation, and shall further include all other persons of one-half or more Indian blood [emphasis added].[25]

In promulgating the IRA, the federal government established, by tacit implication, the concept of *nonrecognized* tribes for which the provisions of the IRA did not apply.[26] The conceptual confusion over what constituted a "tribe" by the federal government led to the Federal Acknowledgement Project in 1978, which provided both an administrative review process and mandatory criteria that must be met for any group seeking acknowledgment as a "tribe" by the federal government.

In the vein of rejecting self-identification as part of Indian policy after the IRA, the Bureau of Indian Affairs instigated a series of "scientific" racial diagnostics based on anthropometric methodology. Even Franz Boas, a founding father of modern anthropology largely known as a cultural relativist who believed that differences in peoples were the result of socio-historical and geographic conditions, asserted that Indians constituted a more primitive form of humanity which helped to explain the dominance of a Native appearance in the offspring of interethnic relationships.

> We find that the Indian type has stronger influence upon the offspring than the white type... expressed in the great frequency of dark hair and dark eyes among half bloods. It may be that dark hair and the wide face are more primitive characteristics of man than the narrow face and light eyes of the whites. Then, it might be said that the characteristics of the Indian are inherited with greater strength because they are older.[27]

Later in his career, Boas was a harsh critic of eugenics, claiming that it was racism disguised as science. But he also turned to anthropometrics to discredit the notion of fixed races. Anthropometrics sought to discern physical differences that were believed to be measurable between ethnic groups. In the late nineteenth century, those carrying out anthropometric studies were particularly preoccupied by how this methodology could define scientific absolutes between groups constructed as distinct races. By the 1930s, officials from the Department of the Interior used anthropometric techniques to determine the blood quantum of individuals identified as American Indians. Anthropometrics fed directly into eugenics studies, since it was applied to the determination of degrees of primitiveness among different human populations.

The *Our Lives* exhibit presents the racial diagnostic photographs, genealogical charts, and determinations of "Indianness" of the Brooks/Locklear family, who were members of the Lumbee tribe in North Carolina. In 1936, Harvard University anthropologist Carl Seltzer relied solely on anthropometric measurements to classify individual Indian blood quantum based on phenotype. When Seltzer conducted his anthropometric study on the Lumbee in 1936–1937, they were officially known as the "Cherokee Indians of Robeson County." Seltzer photographs of the Brooks/Locklear family are part of the racial diagnostics that he compiled, including data on the size, shape, and width of the heads, teeth, skin, nose, lips, and hair of 209 related Lumbees living in the Brooks settlement, Robeson Country, North Carolina. One of his most infamous assessments of their Indianness was the pencil test. Slipping a pencil into his subject's hair, Seltzer determined that if the pencil stayed after mild to vigorous shaking of the head, that person's hair was not Indian. If the pencil slipped out, it had fallen out of real Indian hair. Assessing their physiological characteristics, Seltzer also sought to determine whether the Lumbee whom he tested met the one-half blood quantum required in the IRA. The dubiousness of his science notwithstanding, Seltzer determined that twenty-two individuals did have the physical traits to be certified as one-half blood or more, although inexplicably, within the same Brooks family, siblings with the same mother and father were given different blood quantum designations.[28]

"This 'Indian' stuff has gone far enough"

Continuing further into the *Our Lives* exhibit, visitors are asked to consider the legacy of Virginia's eugenics policies and its impact on individual and collective Native identity. In a section of the exhibit developed in collaboration with members of tribal nations, one of the featured communities, the Pamunkey of Virginia, articulate the legacy of policies implemented by Walter Plecker for their struggle to gain federal recognition as an Indian tribe. In the face of seemingly insurmountable odds, the Pamunkey have maintained a strong distinctive indigenous identity despite four centuries of colonial settlement, and devastations wrought by disease and warfare in the seventeenth century, reservation nullification in the eighteenth century, racialized reclassification in the nineteenth century, and the bureaucratic erasure of their identity as Native peoples in the twentieth century.[29]

From 1924 until 1946, and relying on Virginia's Racial Integrity Act, Walter Plecker uniformly defined as "negro" all Virginia Indian families who had been racialized in the nineteenth century as "free people of color." It was Plecker's opinion that no Virginia Indians were free of African ancestry; their Indianness therefore was considered null and void. Plecker then vigorously worked to further detribalize Virginia's Native peoples, including all divisions of the Monacan,

Chickahominy, Rappahannock, Mattaponi, Nansemond, and Pamunkey by reclassifying them as "Negro."[30] Plecker's methods were simple, direct, and effective. Throughout the 1920s, he campaigned vigorously against Virginia's Native peoples' efforts to be listed as Indians on the 1930 U.S. Census.[31] Throughout Plecker's three-decade career, he sent letters to Virginia's town and county clerks, as well as to physicians, nurses, and school administrators claiming that those seeking to identify as Indians were frauds and criminals:

> Now that these people are playing up the advantages gained by being permitted to give "Indian" as the race of the child's parents on birth certificates, we see the great mistake made in not stopping earlier the organized propagation of this racial falsehood. They have been using the advantage thus gained as an aid to intermarriage into the white race and to attend white schools, and now for some time they have been refusing to register … as negroes, as required…. Some of these mongrels, finding that they have been able to sneak in their birth certificates unchallenged as Indians are now making a rush to register as white. Upon investigation we find that a few local registrars have been permitting such certificates to pass through their hands unquestioned and without warning our office of the fraud.[32]

Plecker focused on the definitions and privileges of whiteness as a means of militating against the possibility of covert genetic incursions by those whom he believed were already tainted with black admixture. For Plecker, "this 'Indian' stuff has gone far enough."[33] If Virginia Indians continued to insist on perpetrating racial fraud, they also faced felony charges punishable "by confinement in the penitentiary for one year."[34] The state's "opportunistic" Indians, not the "feebleminded" or the criminals, bore the brunt of his racist vitriol, and proved to be the most convenient vehicle with which to make his point regarding the pitfalls of social degeneracy through racial contamination. Therefore, it became the imperative of every state bureaucrat to the humblest health care worker to take heed, since "one hundred and fifty thousand other mulattoes in Virginia [were] watching eagerly the attempt of their pseudo-Indian brethren, ready to follow in a rush when the first have made a break in the dike."[35]

The irony of relying on census records from the eighteenth and nineteenth centuries with listings of surnames associated with the Monacan, Pamunkey, Mattaponi, Upper Mattaponi, Nansemond, Rappahannock, Chickahominy, and Eastern Chickahominy tribes seems to have been lost on Plecker, who sought to reclassify and thus detribalize all Virginia Indians as black. Additionally, Plecker took it upon himself to alter birth certificates issued to Indians before 1924, by providing suspect certificates with this inscription:

> The early records of this State show this group of people are descendants of free negroes… Under the law of Virginia, [subject] is, therefore, classified as a colored person.[36]

Plecker's birth certificate alterations, appeals in the form of pamphlets, newspaper editorials, as well as direct correspondence with county and town clerks proved effective.[37] In 1930, the U.S. Census enumerated 779 American Indians living in Virginia; by 1940, the figure had dropped to 198.[38] For all intents and purposes, when it came to matters of births, marriages, and deaths, the Virginia Bureau of Vital Statistics did indeed recognize only two races – white and black.

Although the state of Virginia repealed the Racial Integrity Act in 1967, the impact of Plecker's efforts continues into the present. Under provisions required for federal acknowledgement as an "Indian tribe," petitioning groups must provide documentary evidence of having been identified as an American Indian community on a continuous basis since 1900.[39] Evidence used to substantiate a group's claim comes primarily from preexisting state and federal records and other legal documents such as birth, marriage, and death certificates. Plecker's policies to legally reclassify Natives disrupted this link leading to the near documentary erasure of Virginia's Native peoples.

Eugenics: A Lasting Legacy

The *Our Lives* exhibit at the National Museum of the American Indian highlights racial dynamics that informed and continue to inform narratives of the Southeastern Native historical experience. The lasting legacy of eugenics on Native peoples of the Southeast becomes clearer after excavating the tensions between tribally based definitions of Indianness and those ascribed by state and federal governments. The legacy of eugenics-based public policy and social attitudes during the early twentieth century has been the near documentary erasure of Native peoples in the Southeast. Just as eugenicists such as Plecker turned to science for answers to a perceived problem of miscegenation, newly developing genetic tests touted to identify one's "racial ancestry" signal the latest trend in the racialization of identity. Similar to Galton's concept of fractional inheritance, genetic tests perpetuate biological essentialism and racial classificatory systems that had already begun the process of detribalization. This blood-based assumption of race is entrenched in the discourse of Native identity, resulting in the reification of "blood" as a documentable determinant of one's Indianness. Charted historically, answers to questions concerning "who is Native" and "what constitutes a tribe" reflect both changing and inherited perceptions and political expediencies available to those in power.

In arrogating to themselves the power to identify and define Native peoples in the Southeast, eugenicists such as Plecker helped to promulgate public policies that led to Native displacement and detribalization. For Native peoples such as the Pamunkey, the legacy of eugenics continues to exert itself in the tribe's struggle to gain federal acknowledgement. Because of the acknowledgement process requirement of detailed records of tribal ancestry, Virginia's Native peoples argue that they were subject to "paper genocide" given the lethal combination of Virginia's old race laws and the Racial Integrity Act of 1924 that classified Indians a "'mongrel,' 'colored' or 'negro,' thus making it all but impossible to satisfy the [Bureau of Indian Affairs] requirement."[40] The irony of their status as nonfederally recognized Indians, as well as the unrecognized status of other Virginia tribes, is all the more disturbing given that 2007 marks the four-hundredth anniversary of the founding of Jamestown.

Similar to public exhibits, commemorations of significant historical events all too often serve as a trigger to *memory*, if not history, in all its complexity and contextuality. Given the public nature of historical commemorations, how are we to incorporate reflections of the past's imprint on our own present when some of the descendants of those who made the past *history* are themselves not recognized in the present? Virginia's Native peoples have had one of the longest-enduring relationships with various colonial powers, including the United States, yet the federal government does not recognize them as Native peoples. One is reminded of Felix S. Cohen's admonition,

> It is a pity that so many Americans today think of the Indian as a romantic or comic figure in American history without contemporary significance. In fact, the Indian plays much the same role in our society that the Jews played in Germany. Like the miner's canary, the Indian marks the shift from fresh air to poison gas in our political atmosphere; and our treatment of Indians, even more than our treatment of other minorities, reflects the rise and fall in our democratic faith.[41]

Whether visiting the *Our Lives* exhibit or commemorating past events, we should be mindful and consider: What is it that we have failed to recognize and in so doing, failed to understand? One of the tasks that stand before us is to continue to uncover, contextualize, and integrate this and other neglected narratives of the Native experience and thereby foster the development of recognizable tribally defined identities.

Notes

1 Established in 1989 by an Act of Congress, the new museum is dedicated to the preservation, study, and exhibition of the life, languages, literature, history, and arts of the Native peoples of the Western Hemisphere. For a discussion and analysis of the significance to public history and commemoration of the National Museum of the American Indian, see the special review section of the *Public Historian* 28, no. 2 (Spring, 2006), edited by Lisa Jacobson.
2 Margaret T. Hodgen investigates the early modern transition to biologically rooted understandings of race in *Early Anthropology in the Sixteenth and Seventeenth Centuries* (Philadelphia: University of Pennsylvania Press, 1964); See also Stephen Jay Gould, *The Mismeasure of Man* (New York: Norton, 1981); Pat Shipman, *The Evolution of Racism: Human Differences and the Use and Abuse of Science* (New York: Simon & Schuster, 1994); and Ivan Hannaford, *Race: The History of an Idea in the West* (Baltimore, MD: Johns Hopkins University Press, 1996).
3 Unlike the biological mechanisms for inheritance based on the contributing genes of both parents, Galton's notion of fractional inheritance not only failed to define

what "characteristics" would be inherited from parents, grandparents, and so on, but was deeply subjective and reflective of cultural values disguised as science. For an analysis of Galton's notion of fractional inheritance and a thorough investigation into the development of science and the rise of eugenics, see Daniel J. Kevles, *In the Name of Eugenics: Genetics and the Uses of Human Heredity* (Cambridge, MA: Harvard University Press, 1995).

4 Arthur H. Estabrook and Ivan E. McDougle, *Mongrel Virginians: The Win Tribe* (Baltimore, MD: Williams & Wilkins Co., 1926).

5 F. James Davis, *Who Is Black? One Nation's Definition* (University Park: Pennsylvania State University Press, 1991).

6 These questions echo the debate over the very humanity of Native peoples first begun in the sixteenth century by Juan Ginés de Sepúlveda and Bartolomé de las Casas. See Lewis Hanke, *All Mankind is One: A Study of the Disputation between Bartolome de las Casas and Juan Gines de Sepulveda* (Dekalb: Northern Illinois Press, 1994), 67.

7 For a contemporaneous interpretation of the impetus behind Progressive Era reform, see Benjamin Parker DeWitt, *The Progressive Movement; a Non-partisan, Comprehensive Discussion of Current Tendencies in American Politics* (New York: MacMillan, 1925). For classic interpretations, see Richard Hofstadter, *The Age of Reform: From Bryan to F.D.R.* (New York: Knopf, 1955); Samuel P. Hays, *The Response to Industrialism, 1885–1914* (Chicago, IL: University of Chicago Press, 1957); Samuel Haber, *Efficiency and Uplift: Scientific Management in the Progressive Era, 1890–1920* (Chicago, IL: University of Chicago Press, 1964); as well as Daniel T. Rogers' overview of the literature, "In Search of Progressivism," *Reviews in American History* 10 (1982): 113–132.

8 In 1883, the British scholar and cousin of Charles Darwin, Francis Galton, wrote, "We greatly want a brief word to express the science of improving stock... especially in the case of man." See Francis Galton, *Inquiries into Human Faculty and Its Development* (London: McMillan, 1883), 24–25; Nancy L. Gallagher considers the historical _ experience of Vermont's rural population and the devastating impact of eugenics policy in *Breeding Better Vermonters: The Eugenics Project in the Green Mountain State* (Hanover, NH: University Press of New England, 1999), 36.

9 Gallagher, *Breeding Better Vermonters*, p. 34. In 1915, Estabrook sought to improve on Dugdale's study by tracking more that 2,000 additional family members, 1258 of whom lived in the northeast and were reproducing – at a cost to the public of at least two million dollars. Arthur H. Estabrook, *The Jukes in 1915* (Washington, DC: Carnegie, 1916), 85; and Edward J. Larson, *Sex, Race, and Science: Eugenics in the Deep South* (Baltimore, MD: Johns Hopkins University Press, 1996), 20.

10 Richard L. Dugdale, *The Jukes: A Story in Crime, Pauperism, Disease, and Heredity* (London: G. P. Putnam's Sons, 1877).

11 Representative works include Charles B. Davenport's, *Heredity in Relation to Eugenics* (New York: H. Holt and Co.,1911), and Davenport's collaboration with H. H. Laughlin, and Henry H. Goddard, *The Study of Human Heredity* (Cold Springs Harbor, NY: Eugenics Record Office, 1911); and Henry H. Goddard, *The Kallikak Family: A Study in the Heredity of Feeble-mindedness* (New York: Macmillan Co., 1912).

12 Florence Harris Danielson and Charles B. Davenport, *The Hill Folk: Report on a Rural Community of Hereditary Defectives* (Cold Spring Harbor, NY: Press of the New Era, 1912).

13 The 68th U.S. Congress passed what is also known as *The Immigration Act of 1924*, or the *National Origins Act*, ch. 190, 43 Stat. 153; it did so one week before passing the *Indian Citizenship Act of 1924* (Snyder Act) ch. 233, 43 Stat. 253, 8 U.S.C. § 1401(a)(2).

14 For a well-considered treatment of the South's initial resistance to eugenics, seezLarson, *Sex, Race, and Science*.

15 *Laws of 1919*, Chapter 281; *Laws of 1929*, Chapter 34; *Laws of 1933*, Chapter 224; *Brewer v. Valk* (1933) 204 N. Car. 186; and *Laws of 1935*, Chapter 463. See as well,

R. Eugene Brown, *Eugenical Sterilization in North Carolina* (Raleigh: Eugenics Board of North Carolina, 1935), 38–39.
16 One can speculate that individual North Carolina Natives could have been listed as "negro" by the Eugenics Board, except that the state recognized seven distinct Native communities. For example, the Lumbee were recognized as the Croatan Indians of Robeson County in 1885. See *North Carolina General Assembly 1885*, chap. 51.
17 See Jane Lawrence, "The Indian Health Service and the Sterilization of Native American Women," *American Indian Quarterly* 24, no. 3 (2000): 400–419; Brint Dillingham, "Indian Women and Indian Health Services Sterilization Practices," *American Indian Journal* 3 (January 1977): 27–28; James Robison, "U.S. Sterilizes 25 Percent of Indian Women: Study," *Chicago Tribune*, (May 22, 1977); and especially Andrea Smith, *Conquest: Sexual Violence and American Indian Genocide* (Boston, MA: South End Press, 2005).
18 *Brown v. Board of Education*, 347 U.S. 483 (1954). The 1964 Civil Rights Act guaranteed equal access to health programs funded by the federal government.
19 See compiled data from the Biennial Reports of the Eugenics Board of North Carolina, 1934–1968, as well as "Table 16: Operations Performed, by Type of Operation and Race, July 1929–June 1968," p. 30, *Biennial Report of the Eugenics Board of North Carolina*, http://state library.dcr.state.nc.us/iss/Eugenics/EugenicsHistoricData.pdf, January 2007.
20 Arthur H. Estabrook and Ivan E. McDougle, *Mongrel Virginians: The Win Tribe* (Baltimore, MD: Williams & Wilkins Co., 1926).
21 Estabrook and McDougle, *Mongrel Virginians*.
22 See *Virginia Acts of Assembly*, 1924, 534–535.
23 Helen C. Rountree, *Pocahontas's People: The Powhatan Indians of Virginia through Four Centuries* (Norman: University of Oklahoma Press, 1989), 221.
24 *Indian Reorganization Act (IRA)* 1934, 25 U.S.C. §§ 461–479. See as well Francis Paul Prucha, *The Great Father: The United States Government and the American Indians* (Lincoln: University of Nebraska Press, 1984), 321–325.
25 See also C. Matthew Snipp, *American Indian: The First of This Land* (New York: Russell Sage Foundation, 1989). The provision of a minimum blood quantum, as one of the bill's original sponsors explained, was intended to reduce the number of persons "claiming the financial and other benefits of the act. Obviously the line must be drawn somewhere or the government would take on impossible financial burdens in extending wardship over persons of minor fractions of Indian blood" (Congressional Record, reprinted in Wilcomb E. Washburn, *The American Indian and the United States: A Documentary History*, 4 vols. (New York: Random House, 1973), 1972–1973.
26 See Felix S. Cohen, *Handbook of Federal Indian Law* (Charlottesville, VA: Michie, BobbsMerrill, 1942), 268.
27 Franz Boas, *The Half-Blood Indian: An Anthropometric Study* (New York: D. Appleton and Co., 1894).
28 See Carl C. Seltzer, "A Report on the Racial Status of Certain People in Robeson County, North Carolina," June 30, 1936. [NARA. RG 75, Entry 616, Box 13–15, North Carolina].
29 See Rountree, *Pocahontas's People*, 222–223.
30 In 1935, Plecker gave the keynote address at the Third International Conference of Eugenics where Ernst Rudin, who would help author Hitler's eugenics laws, was in attendance. Several years later, Plecker wrote a complimentary letter to Walter Gross, Germany's Director of Human Betterment and Eugenics, in order to congratulate him on sterilizing 600 children who were the offspring of German mothers and black fathers in Algeria (*The Virginian Pilot*, August 18, 2004).
31 Personal Papers of Calvin L. Beale, "letter of January 14, 1925," and "letter of November 15, 1926." Cited in Rountree, *Pocahontas's People*, 226.

32 See Walter Plecker, "Letter to Local Registrars, Physicians, Health Officers, Nurses, School Superintendents, and Clerks of the Courts," January 1943, http://www.vcdh.virginia.edu/encounter/projects/monacans/Contemporary_Monacans/ letterscan.html (accessed December 2006).
33 Rountree, *Pocahontas's People,* 231.
34 "An Act to Preserve Racial Integrity," *1924 Virginia Acts,* Chapter 371.
35 Plecker, "Letter to Local Registrars," January 1943, http://www.vcdh.virginia.edu/encounter/projects/monacans/Contemporary_Monacans/ letterscan.html (accessed December 2006).
36 See "W.A. Plecker, M.D.," 27 February, 1942, *James R. Coates. Records Concerning the Ancestry of Indians in Virginia, 1833–1947.* Accession 31577 (Richmond: Virginia State Library); cited in Rountree, *Pocahontas's People,* 232.
37 Walter Ashby Plecker's publications include *Eugenics in Relation to the New Family and the Law on Racial Integrity* (Richmond: D. Bottom, Superintendent Public Printing, 1924); *The New Family and Race Improvement* (Richmond: Virginia Bureau of Vital Statistics, 1925); and "Racial Improvement," *Virginia Medical Monthly* (November 1925). For a detailed examination of Plecker's efforts, see J. David Smith, *The Eugenic Assault on America: Scenes in Red, White, and Black* (Fairfax, VA: George Mason University Press, 1992), 59–100.
38 U.S. Bureau of the Census. The 15th Census of the U.S.: 1930, "Virginia" (Washington, DC); U.S. Bureau of the Census. The 16th Census of the U.S.: 1940, "Virginia" (Washington, DC).
39 The regulations governing the federal acknowledgment of Indian tribes can be found in the Code of Federal Regulations, Title 25, Volume 1, Section 83 [revised as of April 1, 2001].
40 John Cramer, "Va. Indians Still Hunt Federal Recognition" *Roanoke Times* (January 6, 2006), http://www.roanoke.com/news/roanoke/wb/wb/xp-47211 (accessed January 11, 2007).
41 Felix S. Cohen made his comparison of North America's Native peoples to the miner's canary twice. This second version appeared in "The Erosion of Indian Rights, 1950–1953: A Case Study in Bureaucracy," *Yale Law Journal* (1953); cited in "Getting a bead on Felix Cohen's 'miners' canary'," *Indian Country Today* (August 31, 2006), 1.

PART II
Perspectives

4

AFRO-NATIVE REALITIES*

Sharon P. Holland and Tiya Miles

Introduction: The Urgency of Be(Longing)

The image of a little red book is imprinted on the minds of many a present-day scholar laboring in the field of Afro-/Native Studies. One of the co-authors of this essay first encountered the tome as a young woman visiting potential colleges with her mother in the late 1980s. In a small black-owned bookstore near Spelman and Morehouse Colleges in Atlanta, that little red book, *Black Indians: A Hidden Heritage*, was propped up and facing out on a top shelf. Its cover featured an African American man and Native American man standing shoulder to shoulder as they stared back at the camera, bodies stiff, faces alive with enigmatic expression. The bookstore owner explained that *Black Indians*, published in 1986, was a sleeper hit, popular especially with prisoners who wrote in to request copies by mail. Embraced by an African American reading public consisting of multiple sub-groups, historian William Loren Katz's book met a more skeptical Native American and general audience. Katz's celebratory survey of African American and Native American historical relations (intended at first for a juvenile readership) was apparently viewed by many who encountered it as a contradiction in terms. Katz writes in a new preface to the 25th anniversary edition that one characteristic response to the book was: "There were *not!*"—a direct refusal to entertain the notion represented by his title.[1] "Black" and "Indian" were terms that seemed to cancel one another out in the minds of some potential readers. These two words and the conceptualizations that accompanied them appeared divorced to these critics—as areas of personal and community identity as well as fields of intertwined intellectual inquiry. "Black Indian" was therefore a category akin to ghost in the 1980s, barely visible, threatening yet incredible, haunting the edges of the American imaginary.

* Note: The piece is a reprint that appears in Robert Warrior, ed., *The World of Indigenous North America*, published by Routledge, ISBN 9780415879521.

The incredulity of this public reaction was due in no small part to the logical establishment of separate historical literatures about Native Americans and African Americans since the turn toward production of scholarly work on black and native people in the 1960s. It was also due to the long tradition and ongoing tendency for major works in African American history and Native American history to analyze these groups in relation to white historical actors and the U.S. government rather than in relation to other groups of color. Pernicious cultural definitions of race, too, structured this divide, as blackness has been capaciously defined by various state laws according to the legendary one-drop rule, while Indianness has been defined by the U.S. government according to the many buckets rule. While one drop of black blood makes a person black in American legal and commonsense culture, Indianness can only be demonstrated by an overwhelming amount of Indian blood, quantified in the formula of blood quantum. In real terms set forth by American officials, "Black" did, in fact, cancel "Indian" out. Anthropologist Circe Sturm has effectively described this difference between systems of racial categorization for blacks versus native people, writing: "The rules of hypodescent played out in such a way that people with any degree of African American blood were usually classified exclusively as Black." In Sturm's summary of the practical outcomes of this logic, a Black/Indian multiracial combination yields "Black," while a White/Indian multiracial combination yields "Indian." One of Sturm's informants, a Cherokee freedmen descendant, put it even more succinctly: "This is America where being to any degree Black is the same thing as being to any degree pregnant."[2]

Within this charged racial context in which a black person could never be Indian, Katz's bold, provocatively titled and fast-paced book made a significant splash. *Black Indians* was the first popular treatment of black-native interrelations and identities. It was not, however, the first important publication on this topic. Before Katz entered the field, and as early as the 1920s and 1930s, African American studies scholars and, later, Native American studies scholars, were delving into this subject area and producing substantial work. While this essay is not intended to be a comprehensive literature review, we do seek to briefly situate scholarship at the black-native nexus in the intellectual genealogy to which it belongs.[3]

We locate the birth of a field in Afro-/Native studies in the *Journal of Negro History*, where towering historians Carter G. Woodson, Kenneth W. Porter, and James Hugo Johnston published a series of articles on black and native interconnections. Carter G. Woodson's "The Relations of Negroes and Indians in Massachusetts" (1920) produced the well-known quotation, "One of the longest unwritten chapters of the history of the United States is that treating of the relations of the Negroes and the Indians." James Hugo Johnston's wide-ranging "Documentary Evidence of the Relations of Negroes and Indians" (1929) offered a survey of key themes and extant primary sources. And Kenneth Wiggins Porter's "Relations between Negroes and Indians within the Present Limits of the United States" (1932), as well as his "Notes Supplementary" to that article (1933), rounded out Johnston's documentary project.[4] Historian Laura Lovett has argued that these early scholars investigated black and native ties as a means of disrupting the Eugenics movement and disproving related claims about racial fixity and black inferiority.[5] In a move that would broaden the methods for Afro-/Native Studies to include an ethnohistorical approach, Laurence Foster then wrote an influential dissertation on *Negro-Indian Relationships in the Southeast*. Published in 1935, the work was based on historical research and anthropological interviews that Foster had conducted in Oklahoma, Texas, and Mexico.[6] Following in the same vein, Kenneth Wiggins Porter returned to this subject area, reexamined Foster's primary sources, and began to conduct interviews with descendants of the Black Seminoles in Texas, Oklahoma, and Mexico. Porter's first Black Seminoles articles appeared in the 1940s in the *Journal of Negro History*.

Porter's scholarly contributions culminated with the posthumous publication, 15 years after his death, of *Black Seminoles: History of a Freedom-Seeking People* (1996).[7] During the same period that Porter was conducting interviews, pioneering black anthropologist William Shedrick Willis performed some of the first ethnographic research on the crossings of African and Native peoples. His scholarship during the late 1950s and early 1960s helped broaden the field of Afro-Native Studies with notable articles like "Divide and Rule: Red, White, and Black in the Southeast," in the *Journal of Negro History*.[8] In the 1970s, historians and ethnographers began to publish a series of works looking at the confluence of black and Indian communities. In 1974, Gary B. Nash published *Red, White and Black: The Peoples of Early North America* (1974), which has a long segment on black/Indian relations. In the late 1970s, three key texts focusing on Cherokee/black relations appeared: Rudy Halliburton Jr.'s *Red Over Black: Black Slavery Among the Cherokee Indians* (1977); Daniel F. Littlefield Jr.'s *The Cherokee Freedmen: From Emancipation to American Citizenship* (1978); and Theda Perdue's *Slavery and the Evolution of Cherokee Society, 1540–1866* (1979). Other important works of the late 1970s and early 1980s included Karen I. Blu's *The Lumbee Problem: the Making of an American Indian People* (1980), J. Leitch Wright's *The Only Land They Knew: the Tragic Story of the American Indians in the Old South* (1981), and James Merrell's "The Racial Education of the Catawba Indians," published in the *Journal of Southern History* (1984).[9] In 1986, as the field continued to grow, William Loren Katz's popular survey, *Black Indians*, appeared. Two years later, anthropologist Jack D. Forbes published a preliminary version of what would become the important work: *Africans and Native Americans: The Language of Race and the Evolution of Red-Black Peoples* (1988, 1993).[10] Forbes' study was a watershed moment for the field, as his exhaustive research into archives at "contact" proved that words like "mulatto/a," "colored," "black," or even "Indian" didn't often represent or reflect adequately the identities of the peoples who fell under the surveyor's pen. More often than not, these words were used interchangeably and according to prevailing law and custom of the various Dutch, French, English, Spanish, or Portuguese colonial powers. Forbes's work was followed by anthropologist Rebecca Bateman's expansion of the field into the Caribbean, with her article "Africans and Indians:

A Comparative Study of the Black Carib and Black Seminoles," published in the journal *Ethnohistory*, as well as by Kevin Mulroy's *Freedom on the Border: The Seminole Maroons in Florida, the Indian Territory, Coahuila and Texas* (1993), which sharpened the lens of previous work produced on Black Seminoles by Kenneth Porter and Daniel F. Littlefield.[11] Soon thereafter, Donal F. Lindsey produced the first educational history in the field, *Indians at Hampton Institute, 1877–1923* (1995). After decades dominated by historical and anthropological approaches, literary analyses also began to appear, most notably in Sharon Holland's early article "If You Know I Have a History, You Will Respect Me: A Perspective on Afro-Native Literatures," *Callaloo* (1994).[12] This work was anthologized in Jonathan Brennan's significant contribution, *When Brer Rabbit Meets Coyote: African-Native American Literature* (2003).

Ten years after the publication of Katz's and Forbes' work, and perhaps not by coincidence, an eminent figure in Native American Studies gave a relevant keynote lecture on "The Future of American Indian Histories" as part of "Meeting Ground," the 25th anniversary conference of the Newberry Library's D'Arcy McNickle Center for American Indian History. Vine Deloria Jr., who himself had compared and contrasted Native American and African American treatment and protest strategies in *Custer Died for Your Sins: An Indian Manifesto* (1969) and in *We Talk, You Listen* (1970), declared in 1997 that Native American history should include extensive comparative work in the future.[13] After 2000 (and perhaps in response to a greater awareness of mixed-race identities spurred by the multiracial movement that sought a new census category for that year), a fourth generation of scholarly work on Afro-Native peoples and African-American and Native American crossings began to emerge in the form of edited collections: James F. Brooks's *Confounding the Color Line: the Indian-Black Experience in North America* (2002), Jonathan Brennan's *When Brer Rabbit Meets Coyote: African-Native American Literature* (2003), Terri Straus's *Race, Roots, and Relations: Native and African Americans* (2005) and Tiya Miles and Sharon Holland's *Crossing Waters, Crossing Worlds: The African Diaspora in Indian Country* (2006) appeared in rapid succession.[14] Literary treatments gathered momentum within these edited collections as well as in monographs such as Joanna Brooks' *American Lazarus: Religion and the Rise of African-American and Native American Literatures* (2003). In 2004, research librarian Lisa Bier published her exhaustive annotated bibliography, *American Indian and African American People, Communities, and Interactions*, cataloging the multi-disciplinary contributions that were shaping a flourishing field.[15] The list of monographs published since 2000 is lengthy and robust, and includes the following notable works: Circe Sturm, *Blood Politics: Race, Culture, and Identity in the Cherokee Nation of Oklahoma*; Rachel Buff, *Immigration and the Political Economy of Home: West Indian Brooklyn and American Indian Minneapolis, 1945–1992*; Rosalyn Howard, *Black Seminoles in the Bahamas*; Tiya Miles, *Ties That Bind: The Story of an Afro-Cherokee Family in Slavery and Freedom*; Claudio Saunt, *Black, White, and Indian: Race and the Unmaking of an American Family*; Cynthia Cumfer, *Separate Peoples, One Land: The Minds of Cherokees, Blacks,* and Whites on the Tennessee Frontier; Gary Zellar, *African Creeks: Estelvste and the Creek Nation*; Celia Naylor, *African Cherokees in Indian Territory: From Chattel to Citizens*; Fay A. Yarbrough, *Race and the Cherokee Nation: Sovereignty in the Nineteenth Century*; Kim Cary Warren, *The Quest for Citizenship: African American and Native American Education in Kansas, 1880–1935*; David A. Chang, *The Color of the Land: Race, Nation, and the Politics of Landownership in Oklahoma, 1832–1929*; Malinda Maynor Lowery, *Lumbee Indians in the Jim Crow South: Race, Identity, and the Making of a Nation*; Brian Klopotek, *Recognition Odysseys: Indigeneity, Race, and Federal Tribal Recognition Policy in Three Louisiana Indian Communities*; Angela Pulley Hudson, *Creek Paths and Federal Roads: Indians, Settlers, and Slaves and the Making of the American South*; Barbara Krauthamer, *Black Slaves, Indian Masters: Slavery, Emancipation, and Citizenship in the Native American South*.[16]

This renaissance was furthered by an academic and community gathering in 2000 titled "Eating out of the Same Pot," but known simply as "The Dartmouth Conference," as well as by symposia that followed at the University of Kansas and the University of New Mexico, by a Red-Black Scholars listserv launched by a graduate student at Michigan State University, and by a documentary film, *Black Indians: An American Story,* that was largely recorded on site at the Dartmouth Conference.[17] Many of these studies have taken as their point of focus the so-called "Five Civilized Tribes" of the South—Cherokees, Creeks, Choctaws, Chickasaws, and Seminoles—which engaged with the institution of black slavery and hence had sizeable black populations. Increasingly, scholars in the field are pushing past the geographical boundaries of the South, of Indian Territory, and even of the Caribbean, to study locations like New England, the Midwest, and the Rocky Mountain West. Creative intersectional treatments of black-native histories and cultures are continually being produced by emerging, as well as established, scholars in African American Studies, Native American Studies, American Studies, and Comparative Ethnic Studies. These scholars bring to their work a keen interest in questions of race, gender, class, sexual relations, land, tribe, nation, colonialism, and power inspired by critical cultural, racial, feminist, and colonial theories. Their composite projects advance a now undeniable field of inquiry in Afro-/Native Studies, which continues with gale force to probe a range of topics like Indian enslavement and slaveholding; gender and sexualities in black and native lives; family-making and adoption practices; recovered texts by writers of black and native descent; modern Afro-Native subjectivities; trade, economies, and economic interactions; Indians, Jim Crow, and white supremacy; black missionaries and educators in native communities; black and native intersecting intellectual histories, and so on.

Scholars who take up this comparative approach and extend it further into inter-relational and intersectional analyses see a logic and, indeed, an imperative for this work, given the historical reality of multiple and complex cross-cultural, cross-racial encounters in the Americas. Native American Studies shares common questions, then, with African American Studies, Latina/o Studies, Asian American and Pacific Islander American Studies, Women's Gender, Sexuality and Disability Studies—questions about power and oppression, survival and resistance, creativity and love, on these Indigenous lands. There is rich and compelling work to be done at each of these intersections, at the same time that the red-black nexus holds a particular valence in American Studies. As Chicana feminist theorist Cherrie Moraga has put it, these groups were "the first" and "the forced" in processes of American racialization and settler colonialism.[18] Their interconnection—historically, theoretically, and politically—rests on a core relationship to the history of the U.S. as peoples whose combined labor and lands formed the literal groundwork of this nation.

In tandem with provocative new scholarship in history, ethnohistory, and literary criticism, a slate of university courses has appeared. The "Black Indian" or "Afro-/Native" Studies classroom has become almost commonplace in Ethnic Studies and American Studies departments (with the question of what should be placed on syllabi dominating the Red-Black Scholars listserv for a time). It is satisfying, for those who think that American Studies should not be uniformly approached from a Euro-American standpoint, to see these courses on the books. And yet, the Afro-/Native Studies classroom is a vexed and complex space. If our experience is any indication, scholars attempting to produce nuanced work in the field meet, in the classroom, students on an urgent quest. Their quest often stems from a fierce longing for a sturdy, fulsome sense of identity in the face of scrutiny, denial, and exclusion in their families, communities, and campus student groups. They want to know who they are, where their families fit, and whether they belong. These students seeking identity reinforcements are black and also Indian, black claiming Indian, and Indian with the keen recognition of the complexity and hybridity of their own racial and cultural makeup. They fill our classrooms to overflowing, searching for meaning and affirmation, hunting for stories and ancestors. These students' raw desire for self- and group knowledge, and the moving, sometimes tense moments in which they express that desire in class mirror the articulations and performances that often occur in public spaces when scholars in Afro-/Native Studies present their research.

Four generations and many a scholarly book and article later, there is still a longing to belong, a need for visibility, a quest called tribe that is manifested among people who identify as both black and native. That longing is rooted in a history of erasure forced by colonialism, racialization, and enslavement; it is also shaped by equally forceful histories of black pride and native cultural recovery that insist upon policing authenticity and building protective walls. So what would we tell our students who seek but do not find? How would we characterize Afro-Native realities, looking both forward and back? In the introduction to *Black, White and Indian: Race and the Unmaking of an American Family*, the story of the two branches of a mixed-race Creek family, historian Claudio Saunt observes the following:

> Though the subject is often underplayed in history books, race was a central element in the lives of *southeastern* Indians, not just as a marker of difference

between natives and white newcomers but as a divisive and destructive force within Indian communities themselves. This book examines how and why race was such a powerful force in Indian lives. It argues that abiding by American's racial hierarchy was a survival strategy—part *cynical ploy, clever subterfuge,* and *painful compromise.*[19]

We cannot think of a better synopsis of the work we do in Afro-/Native Studies than Saunt's redaction of what is at stake when marginalized peoples come into contact with one another, often making family across the generations in the compromising context of pain and loss.

Historical Intersections: 40 Acres and a Tool

Pain and loss. Slavery and land. These terms map onto and move through one another as perhaps the primary concepts in Afro-/Native Studies. Without a fertile land-base and free labor to work it, the U.S. would not have developed into the prosperous empire that it became. Land was usurped from Indigenous Americans, labor extracted from people of African as well as native descent. For nearly two centuries in early America, Indians and Africans were enslaved together. Historians J. Leitch Wright, Alan Gallay, Christina Snyder, and others have documented the capture, sale, and enslavement of tens of thousands of Native Americans in English and Spanish colonies.[20] Even as an African diaspora was being formed through the dispersal of enslaved blacks across the Atlantic Ocean, an "American diaspora," in the words of anthropologist Jack Forbes, was shaped through the dispersal of enslaved Indigenous Americans.[21] Many of these native slaves were traded to the Caribbean and Europe; some were sold to New England and the upper South. The urban center of Charles Town, South Carolina, was the main locus for the sale of both black and Indian slaves, who stood on the same auction blocks, traveled across the Atlantic on the same ships, and finally ended up in the same urban households or rural plantations.

The shared circumstances of their enslavement led to the intersection of black and native lives. Historian Peter H. Wood observed this merging in his classic study of blacks in South Carolina, writing: "during the proprietary era several thousand Indian slaves still shared the same tasks and the same quarters with Africans from overseas."[22] In the North as well as the South, black and native people formed intimate sexual and familial relationships. Historian Daniel Mandell has shown in his histories of New England that dynamics of the slave trade favored the possession of African men over women at the same time that native men lost numbers due to warfare and mobile work; the result was a trend of intermarriage between black men and Indian women.[23] Examples of black and native couplings have been documented across regions, but many more of these relationships cannot be documented by extant written records. Although interracial intimacy continued within the slave population, enslaved Indians became less visible over time, likely due to the misclassification of slaveowners, who reduced mixed-race slaves to the catch-all category "Negro." This extensive period of spatial and social overlap in the crucible of slavery would form the foundation of an interconnected future despite a separation to come.

By the late eighteenth century, the enslavement of Native Americans had fallen out of fashion in colonial practice and law. Enlightenment thought, the image of the noble savage, and the rhetoric of the American Revolution combined to snuff out the practice. At the same time, the importation of African slaves increased, an ideology of racial difference took hold, and a subset of influential Native Americans in the South began to own black slaves. Many, but not all, Indian slaveholders were the mixed-race children of native mothers and white fathers. They were political leaders of their nations who complied with U.S. government dictates to adopt large-scale farming and American "implements of husbandry," or tools.[24] These leading men sought to increase agricultural productivity and demonstrate their people's level of "civilization" to an encroaching U.S. government that made acculturation the price of protection from U.S. settlers. To do so, they increased their reliance on black slave labor. This was a survival strategy that aimed to prove native rights to land and self-government through capitalistic enterprise and Euro-American principles. And yet the execution of this strategy came at the great expense of black human rights as well as native traditional kinship practices. This was the period in which some native people began to adopt American-influenced notions of racial hierarchy and black inferiority. Native and black histories would seem to have split violently apart by 1800, the year marked by historian James Merrell as a turning point when anti-black prejudice was evident in expressions of the Catawba people of the Carolinas, and Catawbas began to disavow previous marriages and kinship ties with blacks.[25] Nevertheless, close relations persisted between individual black and native people even throughout the period of Indian participation in black chattel slavery. This closeness was, to a large extent, the ugly physical and emotional intimacy shared by master and slave, but also the connection that resulted from the acceptance of some black runaways into native communities, particularly the Seminole nation. When native survival strategies backfired and the U.S. government and settler populace forced Indigenous people off their lands in the era of Indian removal, black and native lives again converged.

A longtime and vehement proponent of Indian relocation, President Andrew Jackson's first State of the Union address in December of 1829 outlined a plan for "removal" of Indians east of the Mississippi and urged Congress to adopt it. In Jackson's view, the removal of eastern Indians to a region west of the Mississippi was "not only liberal, but generous."[26] Historian Mary Hershberger has observed that slavery played a role in the successful passage of the Removal Act, since the 3/5 clause of the U.S. Constitution (which apportioned additional representation in Congress for numbers of slaves owned) increased the voting power of southern whites who craved Indian land.[27] The Indian Removal period, formally launched by the Indian Removal Act (yet informally advanced across U.S. administrations dating back to Thomas Jefferson's presidency), did more than open southern and midwestern lands to white settlement. In the South, the ousting of native people cleared fertile land for an expanding plantation economy that would run on slave labor and produce the lucrative cotton kingdom. Indian land and black labor were tightly interlocked in this nineteenth-century moment of U.S. national (and domestic imperial) expansion. The forced migration of African American slaves occurred in tandem with the expulsion of Cherokees, Creeks, Choctaws, Chickasaws, and Seminoles. At the same time that blacks owned by whites were moved from the Upper South into the Deep South to work these newly opened lands, blacks owned by Native Americans were compelled to move west to Indian Territory with their native owners.

In the Cherokee Nation in particular, the largest slaveholding Indian group, black experience of the Trail of Tears represents an additional layer of meaning and poignancy in this conjoined history: 1,652 people of African descent lived in the Cherokee Nation just prior to removal, comprising 10 percent of the Cherokee populace.[28] Former Cherokee Principal Chief Wilma Mankiller captured the gravitas of this interconnected past in her memoir, where she wrote:

> It should be remembered that hundreds of people of African ancestry also walked the Trail of Tears with the Cherokees during the forced removal of 1838–1839. Although we know about the terrible human suffering of our native people and the members of the other tribes during the removal, we rarely hear of those black people who also suffered.[29]

Despite the lack of attention to black experience in removal records, it is possible to piece together parts of this submerged history. The first Cherokees to leave the Southeast in the aftermath of the ratification of the Treaty of New Echota were affluent, slaveholding political leaders who had signed the agreement. Wealthy families like the Ridges and the Vanns emigrated before 1838, choosing the most fertile sites on which to rebuild their plantations. Black slaves who traveled with these families made the journey mainly by water, arriving in time to clear the land and plant the seeds of their masters' new fortunes. A Cherokee freedwoman named Chaney McNair, who had been owned by three Cherokee families, including the prominent Cherokee statesman William Penn Adair, traced her family line to the removal experience. McNair related to a WPA interviewer: "My parents came from Georgia with the Cherokees. They came by boat I spect."[30] Joseph Vann's dramatic transport of his slaves to Webbers Falls made an impression on the memories of Oklahoma residents interviewed by historian Marguerite McFadden in the early 1900s.[31] McFadden reported:

> It was quite a sight for the people around the falls when Joe Vann's property arrived by steamboat ... There were looks of astonishment and shouts of surprise as boat after boat came into view, some towing barges filled with men, women and children. As the boats drew near the shore the onlookers saw the barges were filled with black people, too many to count.[32]

The first tasks for Vann's enslaved blacks were to clear, plow, and build a replica of Vann's stately, southern manor house.[33] The compulsory sacrifice of black bondspeople's labor made it possible for wealthy Cherokees to rebuild their lives in the West. Blacks held by non-wealthy Cherokees walked the journey along with their owners. Many of these bondspeople were compelled to go by the legal and social structures linking them to their masters. Religious historian Patrick Minges has argued in "Beneath the Underdog: Race, Religion and the Trail of Tears" that other slaves may have preferred to leave with their Cherokee owners rather than remaining in a region now controlled by whites.[34] A single case in the Works Progress Administration (WPA) Slave Narratives indicates that blacks not originally belonging to Cherokees may also have ended up on the trail. Cherokee freedman Milton Starr, who claimed that his master, Jerry Starr, was his father, explained that his mother was wrongfully stolen by Cherokees on the walk. Starr said: "My mother was ... a slave girl picked up by the Starrs when they left that country with the rest of the Cherokee Indians.

My mother wasn't bought, but was stole by the Indians."[35] (Figure 4.1)

In addition to bearing the physical and emotional hardships of the journey, enslaved blacks were enlisted to labor for Cherokees along the way. They hunted, nursed the sick, prepared the meals, guarded the camps at night, and hiked ahead

FIGURE 4.1 Slave house near Talala, Indian Territory, 1900. B. Heye Foundation Collection. Courtesy of the Oklahoma Historical Society, photo no. 14864.

to remove obstructions and ensure the usability of roads.[36] One Cherokee man, Nathaniel Willis, remembered that "My grandparents were helped and protected by very faithful Negro slaves who ... went ahead of the wagons and killed any wild beast who came along."[37] Missionary Daniel Butrick also recorded in his journal the labors and deaths of a handful of blacks in his detachment. One elderly black woman, whose children had recently purchased her freedom, "died in the camps." Her son, Peter, and his wife were then sold to slave speculators. Along the trail, one black man "cut some wood for the night," and a black woman: "our kind Nancy" was "employed ... to wash and [dry] our clothes in the evening by the fire." An unnamed black man died on a February day that also took four Cherokee lives. Butrick wrote: "During this time five individuals have died, viz. one old Cherokee woman, one black man, and three Cherokee children, making in all since we crossed the Tennessee River 26 deaths."[38]

Nearly 4,000 Cherokees died during the eviction, and demographer Russell Thornton has argued that taking into account the decline in the birthrate results in an even larger estimate: a total population loss of 10,090 people.[39] Black slaves and free Afro-Cherokees were among those who lost their lives. Their numbers were smaller than that of the Cherokee non-black population, but their suffering was commensurate. As one former slave of Cherokees, Eliza Whitmire, said in her description of the event: "The weeks that followed General Scott's order to remove the Cherokees were filled with horror and suffering for the unfortunate Cherokees *and* their slaves."[40]

In addition to experiencing removal as co-sufferers, black slaves helped to record the event as witnesses. Two WPA Oklahoma interviewees who had been owned by whites recalled details about the time the Cherokees passed through. Nannie Gordon remembered that

> Master Berry's place was on the Ohio river at Berry's Ferry ... They said when the Georgia (Cherokee) Indians come out to this country ... that lots of them Indians was ferried across the river at the master's place. My father and grandfather helped to tow them over.[41]

And Carrie Davis, whose own family was sold apart by their white master, articulated her moral judgment on the government's treatment of the Cherokees:

> When they was sending the Indians to Oklahoma, I had to stay at the train and serve coffee. I made fifty gallons ... They give Oklahoma to the Indians and now they taking it. The Indians have no rights now.[42]

Blacks and Cherokees were joined in the midst of this tragedy by a series of overlapping trials: the physical realities and hardships of relocation, the necessity of adjusting to a new land, the ideology of white supremacy that rationalized the violation of both native and black human rights, and the linkage of slavery and removal in the U.S. political economy. After the Removal Act had been enforced, white southerners in particular and the American nation as a whole benefited enormously at the expense of displaced native people. The expulsion of Cherokees and other Indian nations cleared the way for the expansion of slavery, a variety of which far surpassed Indian slaveholding in intensity and extent. What had been a "society with slaves" in the native South would become, after the Indians' ouster, a "slave society." To borrow the characterization of historians David and Jeanne Heidler, the institution of American slavery and the event of Indian Removal were, in both cause and effect, "twin evils."[43] (Figure 4.2)

In the aftermath of removal and a devastating American Civil War in which the leadership of slaveholding tribes sided (not without internal conflict) with the Confederacy, U.S. officials punished those nations with the seizure of more land, the imposition of railroads, and the proscription that former slaves had to be adopted as tribal citizens. It was after that same war, of course, that African American ex-slaves in the sea island South were promised the infamous "40 acres and a mule" that never materialized. Land was too valuable to assign to blacks, members of a degraded, racialized labor force. Land was also too valuable to be left in the hands of Indians, also racialized, also marginalized, despite their designation as "domestic dependent nations." Relentless in the pursuit of Indigenous land, the U.S. government soon turned to the policy of allotment, which forced the division of remaining native-held common lands into individual homesteads of 40 acres within larger 160-acre plots. In a telling irony

FIGURE 4.2 Freedpeople operated a store (pictured) during enrollment before the Dawes Commission at Fort Gibson, Indian Territory, c. 1899–1901. Aylesworth Album Collection. Courtesy of the Oklahoma Historical Society, photo no. 15805.

of black and native intersections in U.S. history—blacks were denied the 40 acres of land that Indians were reduced to accepting in the allotment process. In order to distribute these lands, the Congressional Commission headed by Senator Henry Dawes mandated a census of native people. The infamous Dawes rolls categorized Indians by blood quantum, formally inscribing a racial definition of Indianness into U.S. law and tribal government practice. "Excess" lands were then distributed to whites, and a race-based system dominated in which "mixed-blood" Indians could control their own landholdings and "full-blood" Indians were deemed wards in an economic free for all that let loose land speculators throughout Indian Territory. Remaining Indian landholdings dwindled. Native national governments were disbanded and did not begin to recover until the early twentieth century. The road to recovery from colonial oppression is long, rough, and continues unending for Indigenous people. It is the roughness of this road, the toughness of American race ideology, and the painful cost of compromise for both blacks and Native Americans that shapes the persistent suspicion of Afro-Native mixed-race people as well as their urge for belonging. The work of unwriting separate historical narratives and imagining into our awareness the reality of these conjoined pasts as well as the possibilities of an interconnected presence and future is taking place most fruitfully in the arenas of literary and visual culture production (Figure 4.3).

FIGURE 4.3 Captain Archibald S. McKennon interviewing freedmen at Fort Gibson, Indian Territory during the Dawes Commission's enrollment of members of the Cherokee Nation, circa 1899–1901. Aylesworth Album Collection. Courtesy of the Oklahoma Historical Society, photo no. 15813.

Literary Production: Ambiguous Subjectivities

One of the most astute critics of an African-Native literature literary genre is Jonathan Brennan, who notes that it is not easy to categorize the genre because "[it] represents an amalgamation of Native American and African American writing traditions, these literatures can be critically examined within at least four different frameworks: as mixed-race literatures, native American literatures, African American literatures, and African-Native American literatures."[44] How should we then go about the business of introducing the wider public to a literature—a literary tradition—fraught with contradiction, often imbued with the cloying presence of the romantic image, and resistant to categorization? From Paul Cuffe to John Horse, histories of black Indian contributions to American letters have just begun to be remade in the late twentieth and early twenty-first centuries. Scholars now recognize Cuffe (Pequot) as a black Indian subject and contemporary of such Indian writers as Hendrick Aupaumut (Mohican), William Apess (Pequot), Black Hawk (Sauk) and George Copway (Ojibwa), who all wrote autobiographies in the mid-nineteenth century.[45] As scholars look more closely at the discrepancy among evidentiary claims for racial belonging, personal statements about family lineage and narrative approaches to subjectivity embedded in literature from autobiography to memoir, from short story to novel tradition, they find more ambiguity than solid ground.[46] We turn to one very good example of the shift from African-American to African-Native subjectivity through the example of one nineteenth century subject: Elleanor Eldridge.

Although she did not produce an autobiography of her own, Elleanor Eldridge's story was one of the most read throughout the nineteenth century and her tale is an interesting counterpart to that of her male contemporaries. Until recently, Eldridge was considered an African-American woman and domestic worker, but as with other tales of identity in the nineteenth century, Eldridge's life needs to be contextualized in light of the fact that her maternal grandmother was Narragansett. Like Cuffe, Eldridge "struggled repeatedly over [her] rights as an African American and a Native American."[47] The publication of the *Memoirs of Elleanor Eldridge* in 1838 marked a significant moment. Written by distinguished Rhode Island resident Frances Harriet Whipple Green MacDougall (1805–1878), the text chronicles the life, toils, and legal wranglings of one Elleanor Eldridge (1784–?1865),[48] a black and native freewoman who was a white washer, weaver, dairymaid, and entrepreneur.[49] Fifteen years Eldridge's junior, Frances Whipple identified with her subject at some psychological level, despite their difference in color and class. Each of them lost a parent early in life and was forced by adverse circumstances to earn her own livelihood. In girlhood, both Frances and Elleanor worked very hard and were recognized as high achievers. As adults, they supported themselves as independent single women during an age when women's ordained social position was considered to be one of dependency on men.[50]

Indeed, there were eight editions of the *Memoirs* published between 1838 and 1847.[51] During the various publication cycles of the narrative, Whipple would marry (1842) and divorce (1847) her first husband, Charles Green, making her an anomaly in the "Victorian" society of Rhode Island. Despite the paucity of critical attention to Eldridge's narrative, both the *Memoirs of Elleanor Eldridge* (1838) and *Elleanor's Second Book* (1839) were reprinted and widely read in the mid-nineteenth century. The first and only scholar to write a full-length biography of Whipple, O'Dowd notes that the text of Eldridge's *Memoirs* "can be read not only as a biographical narrative, but also as a literary text."[52] The particulars of the literary text are indeed intriguing, if only because their drama is so dependent upon one detail of her *Memoir* that intrigues the contemporary Whipple and piques the interest of her twenty-first century explicators.

Early in the account of Eldridge's life, Whipple reports that

> [h]er maternal grandmother, Mary Fuller, was a native Indian, belonging to the small tribe, or clan, called the Fuller family; which was probably a portion of the Narragansett tribe. Certain it is that this tribe, or family, once held great possessions in large tracts of land; with a portion of which Mary Fuller purchased her husband Thomas Prophet; who, until his marriage, had been a slave.[53]

This detail about Eldridge's mixed heritage not only fuels Whipple's scripting of Eldridge's life, but also provides the nexus for further investigation.[54] Was Eldridge, heralded as one of Rhode Island's most notable *African-American* citizens,[55] also of native descent? This question posed additional queries for us: How to speak to the life of someone who acknowledged, at least to Whipple, her dual heritage? What shape would such an exploration take? How to conduct such research without falling into the quagmire of racial and ethnic authenticity, without justifying ideologies such as blood quantum?[56]

Black and Indian passages in New England have been painstakingly articulated in the work of scholars such as Jean O'Brien, Daniel R. Mandell, and Ann McMullen. In particular, McMullen reads C. Matthew Snipps's catalogue of Census data and concludes that "descent [in the twentieth century] may be more important than tribal membership for many"[57] who identify as American Indian.[58] In other words, an investigation of Eldridge's communication to Whipple *and* Whipple's interpretation of her ancestry recalls ongoing debates in contemporary scholarship on multicultural, ethnic, cultural, and racial communities. McMullen writes that "[i]ntermarriage has reduced the importance of blood quantum somewhat, and being Indian is now more often seen as a matter of descent and community participation, or blood and culture."[59] Mandell's research indicates that the contemporary perception of "Indianness" had its complicated and complicating precedent in attitudes among those who intermarried in southern New England between 1760 and 1880— the period in which Eldridge's African grandfather and Indian grandfather saw their grandchildren move into the nineteenth century. Moreover, Mandell's research exposes the "fundamental flaws of a bichromatic view of racial relations in American history" by offering complicated readings of changing relations among intimately inter-related people such as the Narragansett, the Irish and African-Americans.[60]

This work on Eldridge's life and narrative has its counterpart in the fictional world of African-Native American characters. In the literary tradition, authors like Michael Doris (*Yellow Raft in Blue Water*, 1987), Alice Walker (*Temple of My Familiar*, 1989), Nettie Jones (*Mischief Maker*, 1989), Leslie Marmon Silko (*Almanac of the Dead*, 1991), Toni Morrison (*Paradise*, 1998), Percival Everett (*Watershed*, 2003), Sherman Alexie (*Reservation Blues*, 2005), and Zelda Lockhart (*Cold Running Creek*, 2007) either focus upon Afro-Native characters or cultural and familial intersections to make a point about our ideas of history, heritage, and place. Their characterizations of African and Native American peoples provide a snapshot of the thorny territory of mixed-race heritage. But most importantly, what they remind us of, and what some critics often miss, is that Afro-Native subjectivity is not just about mixed-race identity, but is further complicated by the presence of the nation-state. These peoples are not just mixed-bloods, or "cross bloods" to use Gerald Vizenor's term, but they spring from many nations within a nation. The issues of sovereignty, self-determination, and nation-status become crucially important when recognizing what these characters are attempting to mark in what we have come to call the "historical."

Questioned about the America revealed in *Mischief Makers*, Jones replies that she attempts to portray this country as "a true ethnic melting pot whose temperature is perpetually near the boiling point because most Americans refuse to recognize the beauty in the beast."[61] Blackness is a public secret in the text and Indianness is defined in contradistinction to it. The relationship between the main character Raphael (who can pass for "white") and Mishe, a full-blood Chippewa from northeastern Michigan, is weighted with sensuality and tension. Jones's Mishe is little more than a caricature, whose body is so often oversexualized that he becomes almost mythic and at one point in Raphael's dream appears as a centaur rather than as human. What is also more disturbing is that Raphael, a talented nurse and self-assured woman, after marrying Mishe becomes tied to their domestic life—birthing children, raising them, and sleeping with her husband. But between Mishe and Raphael the tension is most prominently placed in their evaluations of history, and it is evident that in this exchange Jones is searching for the right vocabulary to think through cross blood identity. During what Jones calls Mishe's "Chippewa version of history," Raphael thinks:

> She loved her husband's history lessons almost as much as she loved her daddy's version. She promised herself that one day she was going to tell them about aunt Rosebud, who went to Alaska during the gold rush days. It was her strike that provided the money for her only nephew, Raphael's father, to receive medical training. Aunt Rosebud's money bought a lot of land for him too. Otherwise a lot of Detroit Negroes would not have had use of a hospital. She'd save all of that. For later.[62]

Imparted to Raphael earlier in the text is her father's account of his Potawatomie and Pawnee blood, his service in the Spanish-American War, and the thievery of robber barons accused of swindling Native peoples in Michigan's Upper Peninsula to secure the land's resource of lumber. Here, Raphael equates Mishe's story with her "daddy's version," creating a continuity between histories, implying that each is a strand from the same lock. In this story, the "rush" is reflected as part of African-American success, despite its impact upon native peoples (Nisenan among them) in the region and the doctrine of manifest destiny which helped the encroaching settler culture. Jones indicates that this complex narrative that includes a blackness that needs to be hidden and an Indianness that can rarely be imagined outside of the romantic, somehow shifts in the next generation. Lilly, the daughter of Mishe and Raphael, discovers that she is "[p]artly Negro, partly white, partly Indian," and concludes: "I like being parts of all those people. Makes me a partly of everyone—American."[63]

The idea of contesting what is real and what is romance in fiction about African and Native American crossings is taken to another level altogether in Leslie Marmon Silko's masterpiece, *Almanac of the Dead*. Silko dissolves the efficacy of borders and univocal identities by reaching beyond Laguna Pueblo and back again with an epic novel where death is the principal character of a violent popular culture. *Almanac* centers itself both within and without various communities, as technocrats and corrupt officials meander through the text, as Silko explores the depravity and utter disconnectedness of a contemporary society where irrationality is the dominant narrative. Ultimately, the novel is her attempt to deconstruct Western notions of binary oppositions and to create a space of simultaneity—a process supported by both the way events are told in the text and by Silko's narrative structure, where each story is not a "new" beginning but is meant to be laid beside the others in the text. In a chapter entitled "First Black Indian," we meet Clinton, a homeless Vietnam veteran, who "didn't bow and scrape for no Arizona honkie-trash crackers ... [and] lives alone in a Sears garden shed he bought for himself."[64] After the revolution of black and brown peoples, the obsessively paranoid Clinton plans the next step. Silko writes: "Clinton's first broadcast in the reborn United States was going to be dedicated to the children born to escaped African slaves who married Carib Indian survivors. The first broadcast would be dedicated to them—the first African-Native Americans."[65] If we are to understand Clinton's particular form of "outrage" as legitimate rather than hysterical, then we have to view his diatribes against and attempts to correct history as an attempt to give voice to cross blood existence denied to most in the continual historical recounting of colonial rule and this thing called "conquest." Clinton understands the Vietnam war as a governmental conspiracy; he

> had seen how many dark American faces had been in the Asian war. Clinton had seen the white toads, Lyndon Johnson, and his generals, smacking their lips at all the splattered brains and guts of black and brown men.

> Forces sent to destroy Indigenous populations were themselves composed of 'expendables.'[66]

This picture of war is not unlike the status of the Buffalo Soldiers sent to "protect" land in Oklahoma's Indian Territory from invasion by greedy settlers. Clinton achieves agency and a move toward sovereignty because he can see himself in solidarity and relationship with other oppressed peoples. With his revision of history he is able to create a landscape and a sense of place from a reconfigured geography and historical record of the Americas. The landscape of reality that Clinton builds serves as a temporary repository of his sovereign narrative—a space constantly in flux.

But the news of his Indian ancestry is also in this mix. As Clinton remembers:

> [He] had not got over the shock and wonder of it. He and the rest of his family had been direct descendants of wealthy, slave-owning Cherokee Indians. That had been before Georgia white trash and President Andrew Jackson had defied the U.S. Supreme Court to round up all the Indians and herd them west ... That was why a people had to know their history, even the embarrassments when bad judgement had got them slaughtered by the millions.[67]

In his rather comic way, Clinton understands, interprets, and holds onto his own personal history, no matter how brutal or contradictory. In Clinton, Silko paints the portrait of a new ethnic American, one with a fair amount of anger directed at settler and white culture, but also one capable of seeing how the confluence of history, memory, and circumstance create the *collective* racial narrative that is African-Native life *in* letters.

Visual Culture: Seeing a Circle Unbroken

In 2005, Chicago artist Bernard Williams's solo exhibition, "Legendary Tales," opened in Chicago at the G.R. N'Namdi Gallery in the West Loop. Painted in sweeping brushstrokes, reminiscent of Picasso's abstract art, but figurative nonetheless, the images Williams captured were intended to depict the era of the Buffalo Soldiers, a group of African American mercenaries dispatched to Indian country to quell uprisings in the era of manifest destiny's intensification. In fact, if you ask most Americans what they know of black/Indian subjects, they will most likely refer to these men. Williams's own description of the black West is telling:

> [t]he Buffalo Soldier images also speak to the complex role that blacks have played in shaping the country. The soldiers were instrumental to ending some of the last Native American resistance to the European conquest of the west. I paint these characters as individuals in turmoil. They are not

happy but are proud. Their burden is great. They serve gallantly in the brutal system, only to be cast aside, historically guttered.[68]

The soldier's relationship to Indian nations demonstrates the kind of tension that arises when black and Indian bodies meet, cohabit, and make family. Williams's images of black soldiers and bodies in Indian country arise from the deep and enmeshed histories of slavery and sovereignty in what would come to be the United States.

The artistic and literary rendering of this relationship is equally complex. One particular painting of Williams's is entitled *Black Indian*. What strikes any viewer when looking at this painting is the contrast between its bold strokes and its soft hues. The painting's subject is genderless—neither male nor female, but decidedly African in visage. Unlike most of the other paintings in the series, *Black Indian* has no racialized labels painted into its landscape. But the connections "among slavery, western expansion, imperialism and contemporary Africans [appear] as a circle unbroken."[69] This desire to maintain the connectedness of lives, to imagine a "circle unbroken," is the chief ideology that subtends creative, artistic, and literary endeavors to speak to African and Native American intersections.

In another contemporary manifestation of Black-Indian subjectivity, the character of Otis in John Sayles's *Lone Star* (1996) keeps a small museum ("Black Seminole Museum") in the back of his bar. Sayles's film is ostensibly about the confluence of black, white, Indian, and Mexican peoples in a border town in Rio County Texas and the plot is driven by the discovery of a badge in the desert which leads local law enforcement to puzzle through and eventually solve a 40-year-old murder. We soon find out that race has as much to do with law enforcement as it does with family. Toward the end of the film, Otis gives a tour of his museum to his grandson Chet and we are introduced to John Horse, the black Seminole who negotiated with the Spanish in Florida.

OTIS: That's John Horse. Spanish down in Florida called him Juan Caballo. John Horse.[70]
CHET: He a black man or an Indian?
OTIS: Both. He was part of the Seminole Nation, got pushed down into the Everglades in pioneer days. African People who run off from the slaveholders hooked up with them, married up, had children. When the Spanish give up Florida, the U.S. Army come down to move all them Indian peoples off to Oklahoma.
CHET: The Trail of Tears.
OTIS: They teaching that now? Good.

What Otis does not recall is that John Horse was a slave who obtained his freedom sometime in the mid- to late 1840s when he moved into Mexico. Otis's "hobby" points toward the importance of shared history, even though that history might conjure romantic images of black/Indian unity and freedom during Jacksonian democracy. Moreover, Otis marks the fact that his grandson knows about the Trail of Tears, indicating that he is more than pleased that the American history is inching toward some measure of diversity in its telling. The linked images of buffalo soldiers, a black Seminole warrior, and the black Indian portrait noted above indicate a fascination with black and Indian bodies—a fascination that seems to want to locate itself in a time of war. Such images are often romanticized, as is the Indian subject in Julie Dash's film *Daughters of the Dust* who rides in on horseback to rescue his African American intended from her family's attempt to abandon the Gullah Island and culture for the larger world beyond its shores.

In yet another American independent movie, an Indian presence (called Nobody) shows up in two of Jim Jarmusch's films: *Dead Man* (1995) and *Ghost Dog: Way of the Samurai* (1999). The recurring Indian figure is ghost-like in both films, but particularly in the latter. In *Ghost Dog*, Forest Whitaker *is* Ghost Dog the lone warrior and Mafia assassin self-schooled in the Japanese art of the sword; he is also an urban legend who practices his martial art on his rooftop among the pigeons cared for by the Indian, Nobody, played by Gary Farmer (Cayuga). In one particular scene, gangsters ascend to the rooftop looking for Ghost Dog and encounter Nobody among the pigeons.

MAFIA GUY #1: So what are you, Puerto Rican?
[Nobody does not respond]
MAFIA GUY #2: I think he's some sort of an Indian or something.
MAFIA GUY #1: Yo! What the hell are you?
Nobody: Cayuga.
MAFIA GUY #1: Cayuga? What the fuck is Cayuga?
MAFIA GUY #1: Puerto Rican, Indian, nigger ... same thing! I think we should waste him anyway just to be sure.

In a dialogue that attempts to get at the intersection of American ideas of race and racial confusion, the two aging mobsters in the film lump Indian identity with other non-white peoples. Jarmusch's dialogue points toward the necessity for scholars and creative producers to rethink long-held notions about racial formation in the United States. In addition, the aging Mafia men are clearly angry at Nobody's attempt to become *somebody* other than what they want him to be. The use of profanity in the scene and the racial confusion all indicate that claiming an Indian self, let alone mixed identity, is always hazardous in a national conversation that articulates itself in black and white parts.

Conclusion: Visibility and Reality

The articulations and apparitions of these Afro-Native literary and visual culture treatments consistently return to the past, troubled though it is. Seeking out the historical seems to be a means of binding the various strands of this multivalent experience, of bridging the gaps between personal identity, community definition, and racial categorization. It is perhaps fitting, then, that the most significant cultural project in Afro-Native Studies to date has taken the form of an exhibit that visually narrates the past, intimating links to the present. In 2004 in response to the query of a museum visitor, Fred Nahwoosky and others at the Smithsonian Institution's National Museum of the American Indian (NMAI) formed a working group to begin exploring the topic of African American and Native American lives. As the collaborative effort gathered strength, NMAI joined together with the National Museum of African American History and Culture to launch the exhibit: *IndiVisible: African-Native American Lives in the Americas*, along with a companion book bearing the same title.[71] Coordinated by an interdisciplinary, multiracial team of curators and consultants led by Piscataway scholar Gabrielle Tayac, the exhibit collected and assembled a vast array of family snapshots, historical photographs, historical documents, government documents, and family, as well as national, stories from the U.S. and Latin America. Described in the preface to the companion book as a means of acknowledging "the histories and contemporary lives of our African-Native American brothers and sisters," the aim of the project is indicated by its dualistic (and optimistic) title: IndiVisible. The brainchild of Afro-Choctaw anthropologist Robert Keith Collins, this title suggests the need to illuminate the longstanding merger of black and native lives in response to the cultural invisibility of that experience. Recognition is the object here, and in this the project concurs with early observations made by Vine Deloria Jr., who argued in *Custer Died for Your Sins* that contemporary Indians lack visibility on the American scene. Black Indians, a group doubly marked and also doubly marginalized, are rendered all the more invisible, even within Native (and African) America. The multiple large-scale banners and digital personal testimonies that make up the IndiVisible traveling exhibit vividly capture myriad Afro-Native experiences in the past and present, highlighting the essential presence of these peoples, their social ties, as well as tensions.

The exhibit is studded with images of people who appear to be "black" or "mixed race" behaving and dressing in ways that appear to be "Indian"—seeking, it seems, to prove through the visual realm the existence of legitimized Afro-Native people. The exhibit succeeds stunningly with the sheer volume and quality of its visual representations, and yet the very nature of those images framed as evidence of identity evokes a conundrum that a student raised in an Afro-Native Studies class at the University of Michigan. Is it satisfying, in the end, she wondered, to view photographs of Afro-Native individuals and families in this exhibit when we know that visual expectations of "Black" and "Indian" have played a large role in submerging the existence of Afro-Native people? How can the visual ever prove the existence of a people when the reality of their marginalization rests in the trap of racial strictures, shaped, in part, by image and phenotype? Does not reliance on the visual, on "Indian" looks and ways, reinforce set expectations of what a native person should be? Questions like these from younger generations comprise the *future* work of Afro-Native Studies scholars and cultural producers. The preface to the *IndiVisible* essay collection calls that remarkable project "a beginning." It is indeed one among many beginnings, twists, turns and setbacks in the long, unpredictable journey of black and native relations. We stand on a hill looking forward to the next plateau; forward not down. That is a good thing.

Notes

1 William Loren Katz, *Black Indians: A Hidden Heritage* 1986; reprint (New York: Atheneum, 2012), xi.
2 Sturm, "Blood Politics, Racial Classification, and Cherokee National Identity: The Trials and Tribulations of the Cherokee Freedmen," in James Brooks (ed.), *Confounding the Color Line: The Indian-Black Experience in North America* (Lincoln: University of Nebraska Press, 2002), 223–257, 241.
3 For historiographical treatments of Afro-Native history, see Barbara Krauthamer, "African Americans and Native Americans." Black Studies Center, Schomburg, 1–34, http://gateway.proquest.com.proxy.lib.umich.edu/openurl?url_ver=z39.88-2004&res_ dat=xri:bsc:&rft_dat=xri:bsc:ft:essay:10KRAU, October 22, 2007; Tiya Miles and Barbara Krauthamer, "Africans and Native Americans," in Alton Hornsby (ed.), *The Blackwell Companion to African American History* (Oxford: Blackwell, 2004), 121–139; Tiya Miles and Celia E. Naylor, "African-Americans in Indian Societies," in Raymond Fogelson (ed.), *Handbook of North American Indians*, vol. 14, Southeast (Washington, DC: Smithsonian, 2004), 753–759.
4 C. G. Woodson, "The Relations of Negroes and Indians in Massachusetts," *Journal of Negro History* 5(1) (January 1920): 45; J. H. Johnston, "Documentary Evidence of the Relations of Negroes and Indians," *Journal of Negro History* 14(1) (January 1929): 21–43; Kenneth Wiggins Porter, "Relations between Negroes and Indians within the Present Limits of the United States. Contacts as Allies," *Journal of Negro History* 17(3) (January 1932): 287–367; Kenneth Wiggins Porter, "Notes Supplementary to "Relations between Negroes and Indians"," *Journal of Negro History* 18(3) (July 1933): 282–321.
5 Laura L. Lovett, "African and Cherokee by Choice," in James Brooks (ed.), *Confounding the Color Line: The Indian-Black Experience in North America* (Lincoln: University of Nebraska Press, 2002), 192–222, 207–210.
6 Laurence Foster, "Negro-Indian Relationships in the Southeast," Ph.D. diss., University of Pennsylvania, 1935.
7 Kenneth Wiggins Porter, *The Black Seminoles: History of a Freedom-seeking People*, eds. Alcione M. Amos and Thomas P. Senter (Gainesville: University Press of Florida, 1996).
8 William S. Willis, "Divide and Rule: Red, White, and Black in the Southeast," *Journal of Negro History* 48(3) (July 1963): 157–176.
9 Gary B. Nash, *Red, White, and Black: the Peoples of Early America* (Englewood Cliffs, NJ: Prentice-Hall, 1974). Rudy Halliburton Jr., *Red Over Black: Black Slavery among the Cherokee Indians* (Westport, CT: Greenwood Press, 1977); Daniel F. Littlefield Jr., *The Cherokee Freedmen: From Emancipation to American Citizenship* (Westport, CT: Greenwood Press, 1978); Theda Perdue, *Slavery and the Evolution of Cherokee Society, 1540–1866* (Knoxville: University of Tennessee Press, 1979); Karen I. Blu, *The Lumbee Problem: The Making of an American Indian People* (Cambridge: Cambridge University Press, 1980); J. Leitch Wright, *The Only Land They Knew: The Tragic Story of the American Indians in the Old South* (New York: Free Press, 1981); James H. Merrell, "The Racial Education of the Catawba Indians," *Journal of Southern History* 50(3) (August 1984): 363–384.
10 Jack D. Forbes, *Africans and Native Americans: The Language of Race and the Evolution of Red-Black Peoples* (Urbana: University of Illinois Press, 1993); Jack D. Forbes, *Black*

Africans and Native Americans: Color, Race, and Caste in the Evolution of Red-Black Peoples (New York: Blackwell, 1988).
11 Rebecca B. Bateman, "Africans and Indians: A Comparative Study of the Black Carib and Black Seminole," *Ethnohistory* 37(1) (Winter, 1990): 1–24. Kevin Mulroy, *Freedom on the Border: The Seminole Maroons in Florida, the Indian Territory, Coahuila and Texas* (Lubbock: Texas Tech University Press, 1993); Daniel F. Littlefield, *Africans and Seminoles: From Removal to Emancipation* (Westport, CT: Greenwood, 1977).
12 Donal F. Lindsey, *Indians at Hampton Institute, 1877–1923* (Urbana: University of Illinois Press, 1995); Sharon P. Holland, "'If You Know I Have a History, You Will Respect Me': A Perspective on Afro-Native Literatures," *Callaloo* 17(1) (Winter, 1994): 334–350.
13 Vine Deloria Jr., *Custer Died for Your Sins: An Indian Manifesto* (New York: Macmillan, 1969), and *We Talk, You Listen: New Tribes, New Turf* (New York: Macmillan, 1970).
14 James F. Brooks (ed.), *Confounding the Color Line: The Indian-Black Experience in North America* (Lincoln: University of Nebraska Press, 2002); Jonathan Brennan, *When Brer Rabbit Meets Coyote: African-Native American Literature* (Urbana: University of Illinois Press, 2003); Terri Straus (ed.), *Race, Roots, and Relations: Native and African Americans* (Chicago, IL: Albatross Press, 2005); Tiya Miles and Sharon P. Holland (eds.), *Crossing Waters, Crossing Worlds: The African Diaspora in Indian Country* (Durham, NC: Duke University Press, 2006).
15 Joanna Brooks, *American Lazarus: Religion and the Rise of African-American and Native American Literatures* (Oxford/New York: Oxford University Press, 2003); Lisa Bier, *American Indian and African American People, Communities, and Interactions: An Annotated Bibliography* (Westport, CT: Praeger, 2004).
16 Circe Sturm, *Blood Politics: Race, Culture, and Identity in the Cherokee Nation of Oklahoma* (Berkeley: University of California Press, 2002); Rachel Buff, *Immigration and the Political Economy of Home: West Indian Brooklyn and American Indian Minneapolis, 1945–1992* (Berkeley: University of California Press, 2001); Rosalyn Howard, *Black Seminoles in the Bahamas* (Gainesville: University Press of Florida, 2002); Tiya Miles, *Ties That Bind: The Story of an Afro-Cherokee Family in Slavery and Freedom* (Berkeley: University of California Press, 2005); Claudio Saunt, *Black, White, and Indian: Race and the Unmaking of an American Family* (New York: Oxford University Press, 2005); Cynthia Cumfer, *Separate Peoples, One Land: The Minds of Cherokees, Blacks, and Whites on the Tennessee Frontier* (Chapel Hill: University of North Carolina Press, 2007); Gary Zellar, *African Creeks: Estelvste and the Creek Nation* (Norman: University of Oklahoma Press, 2007); Celia Naylor, *African Cherokees in Indian Territory: From Chattel to Citizens* (Chapel Hill: University of North Carolina Press, 2008); Fay A. Yarbrough, *Race and the Cherokee Nation: Sovereignty in the Nineteenth Century* (Philadelphia: University of Pennsylvania Press, 2008); Kim Cary Warren, *The Quest for Citizenship: African American and Native American Education in Kansas, 1880–1935* (Chapel Hill: University of North Carolina Press, 2010); David A. Chang, *The Color of the Land: Race, Nation, and the Politics of Landownership in Oklahoma, 1832–1929* (Chapel Hill: University of North Carolina Press, 2010); Malinda Maynor Lowery, *Lumbee Indians in the Jim Crow South: Race, Identity, and the Making of a Nation* (Chapel Hill: University of North Carolina Press, 2010); Brian Klopotek, *Recognition Odysseys: Indigeneity, Race, and Federal Tribal Recognition Policy in Three Louisiana Indian Communities* (Durham, NC: Duke University Press, 2011); Angela Pulley Hudson, *Creek Paths and Federal Roads: Indians, Settlers, and Slaves and the Making of the American South* (Chapel Hill: University of North Carolina Press, 2010); Barbara Krauthamer, *Black Slaves, Indian Masters: Slavery, Emancipation, and Citizenship in the Native American South* (Chapel Hill: University of North Carolina Press, 2013).
17 *Black Indians: An American Story*, directed by Chip Richie (Dallas, TX: Rich-Heape Films, 2000), DVD.

18 Cherrie L. Moraga, Foreword, in Cherrie L. Moraga and Gloria E. Anzaldua (eds.), *This Bridge Called My Back: Writings by Radical Women of Color* (1981; reprint, Saline, MI: Third Woman Press, 2002), xv–xxxiii, xvi.
19 Saunt, *Black, White, and Indian*, 4; second emphasis added.
20 Alan Gallay, *The Indian Slave Trade: The Rise of the English Empire In the American South, 1670–1717* (New Haven, CT: Yale University Press, 2002); Wright, Jr., *The Only Land They Knew*. Christina Snyder, *Slavery in Indian Country: The Changing Face of Captivity in Early America* (Cambridge: Harvard University Press, 2010).
21 Jack D. Forbes, *Africans and Native Americans*, 47, 64.
22 Peter H. Wood, *Black Majority: Negroes in Colonial South Carolina from 1670 through the Stono Rebellion* (New York: Norton, 1974), 115.
23 Daniel R. Mandell, "The Saga of Sarah Muckamugg: Indian and African American Intermarriage in Colonial New England," in Martha Hodes (ed.), *Sex, Love, Race: Crossing Boundaries in North American History* (New York: New York University Press, 1999), 72–90; Wright, Jr., *The Only Land They Knew*, 148.
24 Treaty with the Cherokee 1791, Article 14, the Avalon Project at Yale University Law School: http://avalon.law.yale.edu/18th_century/chr1791.asp. (April 13, 2013). Also quoted in Miles, *Ties that Bind*, 35.
25 James Merrell, "Racial Education," 363–384.
26 Andrew Jackson, State of the Union Address, December 6, 1830, in Theda Perdue and Michael D. Green (eds.), *The Cherokee Removal: A Brief History with Documents*, 2nd edition (Boston, MA: Bedford/St. Martin's Press, 2005), 119–120, 120.
27 Mary Hershberger, "Mobilizing Women, Anticipating Abolition: The Struggle against Indian Removal in the 1830s," *Journal of American History* (June, 1999): 1, www.history cooperative.org/journals/jah/86.1/hershberger.html (December 10, 2005), 10.
28 William G. McLoughlin and Walter H. Conser, Jr. "The Cherokee Censuses of 1809, 1825, and 1835," in William G. McLoughlin, *The Cherokee Ghost Dance: Essays on the Southeastern Indians 1789–1861* (Macon, GA: Mercer University Press, 1984), 240, 234.
29 Wilma Mankiller and Michael Wallis, *Mankiller: A Chief of Her People* (New York: St. Martin's Press, 1993), 94.
30 T. Lindsay Baker and Julie P. Baker (eds.), *The WPA Oklahoma Slave Narratives* (Norman: University of Oklahoma Press, 1996), 274.
31 *Census Roll, 1835, of the Cherokee Indians East of the Mississippi and Index to the Roll*, National Archives and Records Administration, micro film T496: roll 1 (Washington, DC, 1960), 3.
32 Marguerite McFadden, "The Saga of 'Rich Joe' Vann," *Chronicles of Oklahoma* 61(1) (1983): 68–79, 73. We first saw this description of Joseph Vann's slaves displayed on the wall at the Chief Vann House State Historic Site; We wish to thank Chief Interpretive Ranger Julia Autry for providing a copy of the source.
33 McFadden, 68, 73.
34 Patrick Minges, "'Beneath the Underdog': Race, Religion and the Trail of Tears," *American Indian Quarterly* 25(3) (Summer 2001): 453–479, 467.
35 Baker and Baker, 408.
36 Theda Perdue, *Slavery and the Evolution of Cherokee Society, 1540–1766* (Knoxville: University of Tennessee Press, 1979), 71.
37 Nathaniel Willis, Indian Pioneer Papers, quoted in Minges, "Underdog," 467.
38 Daniel Butrick, *The Journal of Rev. Daniel S. Butrick, May 19, 1838–April 1, 1839, Monograph One* (1839; reprint, Park Hill, OK: Trail of Tears Association Oklahoma Chapter, 1998), 32–33, 54, 61, 58.
39 Russell Thornton, "The Demography of the Trail of Tears Period: A New Estimate of Cherokee Population Losses," in William Anderson (ed.), *Cherokee Removal: Before and After* (Athens: University of Georgia Press, 1991), 75–95, 91. The number of blacks who died along the Trail of Tears has not been estimated.

40 Eliza Whitmire, in Minges (ed.), *Black Indian Slave Narratives*; also quoted in Minges, "Underdog," 466; italics added.
41 Baker and Baker, 170.
42 Baker and Baker, 104.
43 David S. Heidler and Jeanne T. Heidler, *Indian Removal: A Norton Casebook* (New York: W.W. Norton & Company, 2007), 30.
44 Jonathan Brennan, *When Brer Rabbit Meets Coyote: African-Native American Literature* (Urbana: University of Illinois Press, 2003), 43.
45 See Laura L. Mielke, "'Native to the Question': William Apess, Black Hawk, and the Sentimental Context of Early Native American Autobiography," *American Indian Quarterly* 26(2) (Spring, 2002): 246–270.
46 See Emily Donaldson Field's discussion of literary scholars and their approaches to his narrative in "'Excepting Himself': Olaudah Equiano, Native Americans, and the Civilizing Mission," *Multi-Ethnic Literature of the United States* 34(4) (Winter, 2009): 15–38.
47 Jonathan Brennan, *When Brer Rabbit Meets Coyote: African-Native American Literature* (Urbana: University of Illinois Press, 2003), 21.
48 Whipple recalls that "During her mother's life, it had often been her practice to follow washing, at the house of Mr. Joseph Baker, of Warwick; a daughter of whom, Miss Elleanor Baker, gave her own name to the little one she often carried with her" (21). Vital Records for Warwick indicate that Elleanor Baker married William Tillinghast on March 12, 1797—about the time that Whipple reports the young mistress to whom Eldridge was first indentured left the household. Although both Whipple and then O'Dowd note that Eleanor Eldridge lived to be almost 80, the date of 1845 is still reiterated in popular encyclopedic entries and scholarly essays.
49 Frances Harriet Whipple Green McDougall (hereafter noted as Frances Whipple) wrote the first appeal for Eldridge in 1838, modestly titled *Memoirs of Eleanor Eldridge*. Frances Whipple was quite the iconoclast; she hailed from one of the first families of Rhode Island (the Whipples) and spent much of her life championing the rights of ordinary laborers. FHWGM was familiar with Eldridge because the latter was employed by many of Providence's most prominent citizens—the Greens and the Bakers, to name only two. Eldridge went to work as an indentured servant for the Baker family at the age of 10, and worked at various occupations until her death—exact dates of her death are unknown, as Providence records dating back to 1836 indicate that "Eleanor Eldridge/Eleanor Eldredge" did live at 22 Spring Street at least until 1853. Spellings of Eldridge's name vary in both court and informal documents. We have decided to use "Eldridge," since this is the spelling that previous scholars have utilized. For a more detailed account of Frances Whipple's life, see Sarah C. O'Dowd, *A Rhode Island Original: Frances Harriet Whipple Green McDougall* (Hanover, NH: University Press of New England, 2004).
50 O'Dowd, Sarah C., 21.
51 O'Dowd, 19 (see note 1).
52 O'Dowd, 19, 21. While several encyclopedic collections mention the work and life of Elleanor Eldridge, there are few scholarly treatments of her narrative or her history. See note 12.
53 O'Dowd, 20.
54 We are aware that our investigation of Eldridge's Indian ancestry might convey a bias on our part, as the inquiry into her grandfather's ancestry appears to be under-valued. In essence, we are aware that the assumption works both ways. A search of Providence and Warwick Vital Records indicates that Prophets did indeed live in both towns, as the name appears as early as 1745 and as late as 1852. In his 1883 memoirs, William J. Brown notes that he descends from the Prophet line, a well-known African American family in Providence throughout the nineteenth century (phone interview with Rosalind Wiggins, May 2004). Ironically enough, Brown also

mentions that his Narragansett grandmother bought her African-American husband around 1770, "in order to change her mode of living" (quoted in Mandell, 184, from *The Life of William J. Brown* (Providence, 1883)). Likewise, Sarah Muckamugg moved to Providence where she married Aaron Whipple, "a Negro servant" (quoted in Mandell, 189).

55 O'Dowd notes that Eldridge's name was one of the first of 35 women who were proposed to the Rhode Island legislature for statues honoring their contributions (19).
56 The exhaustive research of Jack D. Forbes has been invaluable to scholars researching the early lives and narratives of people of African and Indian descent in the Americas. In particular, his explication of early court records, census data, ledgers, and ship logs reveals that terms such as "black," "Negro," "colored," and "mulatto/a" did not often correspond accurately to the peoples such terms sought to define. As Forbes concludes, "[t]his is a matter of considerable significance for the scholar seeking to understand the actual ethnic or racial identity of non-white persons in the slave trade, in the American colonies and in the United States over the centuries" (*Africans and Native Americans,* 91).
57 McMullen, 269.
58 See C. Michael Snipp, *American Indians: The First of This Land* (New York: Russell Sage Foundation, 1989).
59 McMullen, 269.
60 Daniel R. Mandell, "Shifting Boundaries of Race and Ethnicity: Indian-Black Intermarriage in Southern New England, 1760–1880," *Journal of American History* (September 1998): 466. This is a superb article that treats complex issues of property, race, gender, and generation in the socio-geo-political context of colonial America. He notes the larger hardening of racial difference with the incursion of Enlightenment thought and shifts in a patriarchal notion of property law and citizenship.
61 Caryn James, "Mischievous Women and Skin-Deep Relationships," review of *Mischief Makers,* by Nettie Jones, *New York Times,* March 1, 1989.
62 Nettie Jones, *Mischief Makers* (New York: Weidenfeld and Nicolson, 1989), 15.
63 Jones, 69–70.
64 Leslie Marmon Silko, *Almanac of the Dead* (New York: Simon and Schuster, 1991), 404.
65 Silko, 410.
66 Silko, 407.
67 Silko, 415.
68 Bernard Williams, "The Black West," exhibition catalogue, *Bernard Williams: Legendary Tales,* G.R. N'Namdi Gallery (New York/Chicago, IL, 2005), 7.
69 Kimberly N. Pinder, "Buffalo Soldier Stories: Bernard Williams Paintings of the West," in Williams, *Legendary Tales,* 4.
70 John Horse also appears in Alice Walker's novel *The Temple of My Familiar.*
71 Gabrielle Tayac (ed.), *IndiVisible: African-Native American Lives in the Americas* (Washington, DC: Smithsonian Institution, 2009). For more about the genesis of this project, see Tayac's introduction to the book.

5

SOUTHERN NEW ENGLAND POW-WOWS, RACE, AND NATIVE AMERICAN IDENTITY[1]

Denene De Quintal

In Southern New England[1] pow wows are a primary way for many Native Americans to establish, maintain, and renew both personal and casual relationships in the area. Since a majority of Native Southern New Englanders do not reside on their reservations pow wows provide annual and localized situations for dispersed individuals to return to their reservations and renew contact with both tribal and family members. In addition, pow wows allow local tribes to interact and establish relationships with Native Americans from more distant communities. In Southern New England pow wows are also events that reveal the underlying concerns about the authenticity[2] of Native Americans in Southern New England and where the perceived incommensurability between "Blackness"[3] and Native American identity is discussed, negotiated, and debated.

"Pow wow," "powwow," "pow-wow" has multiple definitions and spellings in the *Oxford English Dictionary*. Those definitions include:

> **1.** Among North American Indians: a priest, shaman, or healer. **2.** A religious or magical ceremony (especially one with feasting) held by North American Indians; a council or conference of North American Indians. **3.** *colloq.* (orig. *U.S.*). More generally: a meeting, a conference, esp. of powerful people; (also) bustle, activity. **4.** Chiefly *U.S. regional* (*Pennsylvania*). The working of cures; ritual medicine or healing; folk magic. Also: an instance of this; a spell or hex.

Incidentally, the etymology of the word comes from "the Narragansett *powwaw*, Massachusetts *pauwau* American Indian priest, ultimately <proto-Algonquian **pawe·wa* he (who) dreams" (Oxford English Dictionary). "Pow wow" as used in this chapter refers to the gathering of Native people to celebrate a general Native American culture through singing, dancing, socializing, and eating.

There have been many works written about pow wow, its origin and purpose in Native American communities (Arndt 2004, 2016; Browner 2002; Ellis 2003; Ellis, Lassiter, and Dunham 2005). Although pow wow's origin has been contested (Browner 2002), it is thought to have originated in the Northern Plains and transmitted to other tribes through interaction and sharing at intertribal gatherings. Pow wow is a blend of Lakota Old Warrior society procedures, the Anishinaabe Drum Exchange, old age Native American musical practices, and Wild West shows (Browner 2002; Watchman 2005). As an amalgamation of different Native and non-Native traditions, pow wows have become central in presenting Native American cultural identity to the American public.

Pow wow is not simply a celebration of Native American culture. It is a social, cultural, psychological, and economic statement of Native American society within the larger United States society (Ellis 2005, 11). Its premise depends on a universal image of Native American people and a generalized view of Native American culture. Pow wow's ability to incorporate Native Americans from different tribes as well as non-Natives demarcates it as a unifying art form that articulates Native American identity to a wide audience. However, pow wow's ability to present a universal image of Native American people can also blur the demarcation between individual tribes and their distinct cultures, as well as regional differences.

Pow wow's ability to attract participants from multiple tribes and combine different Native traditions has garnered it the label "Pan-Indian." As Clyde Ellis and Luke Eric Lassiter define it, Pan-Indian means "to be a part of a homogenized melting pot of Indian culture" (2005, vii). Pow wow is thought to represent the collapse of individual tribal identity and the generalization of Native American identity (Cook, Johns, and Wood 2005; Ellis and Lassiter 2005; Young 1981). Viewing pow wow as a Pan-Indian event, as previously defined, supports the premise that Native Americans are losing their culture and drawing both on a universal image of Native Americans and a common history to forge a collective identity amongst different Native groups (Cook, Johns, and Wood 2005).

However, the pow wow's interpretation as a demonstration of a homogenized Native identity can be countered by interpreting it as a moment in which "subjects are prompted to calibrate the forms and modes of differences confronting them… [pow wows] mark the site where indigenous persons struggle to inhabit the tensions and torsions of competing to *be* and to *identify* differentially" (Povinelli 2002, 13). Pow wows, as moments in Native people's lives, demonstrate how Native people, by not differentiating themselves from each other, fail in the opinion of some anthropologists, ethnologists, and historians, to fulfill their own alterity or fail to be truly indigenous.

Pow wow's Pan-Indian or generalized cultural characteristics are what allow any tribe to utilize it to celebrate their Native culture. In general pow wows are not tribally or culturally specific, thus any tribe can host a pow wow because they do not have to depend on their own tribe's cultural traditions to execute it (Gilley 2005, 225). Pow wow's format has become standardized making it transferrable to tribes that have never held a pow wow before (Toelken 1991). For those tribes who have lost aspects of their culture, pow wow—which projects a generalized notion of Native identity, allows them access to a public Native American identity. This public identity allows them access to the non-Natives who desire to participate in Native cultures through events such as pow wows. Tribes can welcome non-Natives into their communities and display their connection to a Native American identity by utilizing pow wow's visual and social representations of Native American traditions, while not depending on their own specific traditions. Pow wows also provide a common ground for tribes to commune with each other by blurring the cultural differences between tribal groups.

Pow Wowing and Cultural Communications

A reoccurring argument in pow wow scholarship is that pow wows are events that unify diverse tribes by focusing on the commonalities found between tribes instead of their diversities (Mattern 1996). Mark Mattern argues that pow wows also provide a "public arena for negotiation of differences and disagreements" about American Indian identity (1996, 183). In his article he contends that at pow wows, gender, religion/secularism, and relationships between Indians and non-Indians are debated when they come into conflict with established practices. I contend that in Southern New England, another aspect in the debate about Native American identity at pow wows is the authenticity of tribes based on their race and physical appearance. At the time that I conducted my research three of the largest contest pow wows in the East were the Mohegan Wigwam Pow Wow, the Mashantucket Pequots' Schemitzun: Feast of Green Corn and Dance, and the Shinnecock Pow Wow, which occur(red) in sequential, weekends beginning in August.[4] These pow wows, especially Schemitzun, attracted large numbers of Indians from Western tribes, such as the Apaches, Navajos, and Sioux. They also became areas of cultural contestation between tribes and amongst tribal members.

Schemitzun, in its original incarnation, was one of the most controversial pow wows. The Pequots[5] received a lot of criticism about the way they adapted pow wow into the local Native community and how this impacted opinions about the authenticity of tribes in the area. In this chapter, when I refer to "Schemitzun" I am referring to the large festival which was cancelled in 2009, due to loss of casino revenue and depletion of the tribe's wealth. Schemitzun still exists today but in a smaller format, with less participation from Western tribes.

For almost 20 years, the Pequots hosted Schemitzun, one of the largest pow wows in the United States. Schemitzun's size, prize money, and the amount of people it attracted was legendary (Adams 2002; Hatoum 1999, 48). Held under a large tent which seated close to one thousand people, it attracted hundreds of Indians from tribes across the United States, Canada, and Latin America by offering some of the largest monetary prizes on the pow wow circuit. The prize money decreased over time, but in 2008, dance contest winners respectively received for 1st place 1,500 dollars, 2nd place 1,200 dollars, 3rd place 1,000 dollars, and 4th place 800 dollars, and the event still drew many competitors.[6] The ability to win large amounts of prize money and the notoriety that was awarded with winning made traveling to Schemitzun a lucrative investment for talented individuals.

First and foremost, Schemitzun[7] was the Pequot pow wow. The cultural identity of this tribe was emphasized above all others in this venue.[8] Before it was cancelled, the larger Schemitzun was used to address the concerns of non-Natives as well as Western Indians about the credibility of the Pequots as a Native tribe because of their appearance and mixed heritage. By hosting a large pow wow that attracted a large number of Indian tribes, the Pequots used the history as well as the physical appearance of other tribes to "struggle against non-native images of them, sometimes…adopting aspects of Plains Indian culture to meet non-native expectations, all the while upholding their local Indian identity" (McMullen 1996, 54). Schemitzun, for the Pequots, represented the opportunity to emphasize their Indian heritage by linking the tribe to other Indians who physically resembled the part,[9] and to deflect questions about why some of their tribal members did not.

Ann McMullen suggests that pow wows as Pan-Indian events "allowed native people to be recognized but simultaneously created a generic Indian culture that masked local specifics," which in the Pequot case could dispel the sentiments that they were not a real Indian tribe (McMullen 1996, 57). Hosting and even participating in a pow wow allowed the Pequots to "create [their own] versions of history by pulling together surviving traditions and reclaimed traditions, reinterpreting written histories, and setting local tribal history within national or regional settings" (1996, 60). By grafting their own history onto the history of more readily recognizable Indian traditions, the Pequots were able to challenge notions about their Indian identity being inauthentic (Hatoum 1999, 49).

By hosting Schemitzun, which attracted Indians who "looked" like the dominant Indian stereotypes, the Pequots were suggesting, however subtly, to the general public that they were accepted by other Indians as Indians. McMullen argues that the Narragansetts[10] and the Pequots

> both instituted larger pow-wows with considerable dance prizes to attract western Indians. Members of the public saw the Narragansett and Pequot participating in cultural solidarity with western Indians… [it helped] advance their sovereign rights (including the right to build casinos) and achieve recognition by non-Indians.
>
> *(McMullen 1996, 70)*

In addition, having a large number of Indians from other tribes attend Schemitzun helped the Pequots utilize a "generic" Indian identity, which allowed the Pequots to challenge public opinion that they were not Indians because some of them appeared Black.[11]

Many tribes including the Pequots have been successful in grafting their history on to that of Western Indians for either economic or political purposes (Cook, Johns, and Woods 2005; Ellis and Lassiter 2005; Goertzen 2001, 2005). However, the Pequots have been unsuccessful in preventing feelings of resentment amongst local Natives as well as Western Indians created by their use of pow wow to promote their Native American identity (Fromson 2003). Toelken argues that one duty of the host tribe "is to provide occasions for the expression of tribal identity (including their own) but in a way that will not place undue attention on any particular one" (1991, 148). Since its inception, Schemitzun has been controversial to many Native people in Southern New England because Pequot identity, as well as local tribal identities, has been underrepresented. Many Southern New England Natives viewed the pow wow as a tribute to Western tribes, because of its emphasis on Western identity. Although Schemitzun's subtitle, "Feast of Green Corn and Dance," references the non-pow wow traditional harvest dances that were once widespread throughout the Eastern Woodlands and absent in Western tribes, these dances were not performed at Schemitzun (Witthoft 1949). Instead, the dances focused on Western dances such as Grass, Jingle Dress, and Fancy Shawl. Western vendors were featured, thus the food, clothing, and dance styles of Western tribes were on exhibit. Although Eastern Native customs were accessible, they were suppressed in favor of Western customs at Schemitzun.

Northeastern tribes had to petition the Pequots to include Eastern dance categories. They encountered resistance for many years forcing many Easterners to dance in Western categories or not to participate at all.[12] A Narragansett woman mentioned that she hated attending Schemitzun because it was so "Westernized," meaning that it did not focus on the traditional dances and customs of Eastern people, but on those of Western tribes. She suggested that this was one of the reasons why local Indians were so frustrated with the Mashantuckets. She said that many local Indians felt that Schemitzun, which attracted so many Native and non-Native outsiders, could be used to teach people about Eastern Woodland traditions, but instead it was used to glorify Western traditions.

In order to mollify local tribes and perhaps teach local non-Natives and Western Indians about Eastern traditions, Schemitzun added Eastern dance categories like the men's Eastern War Dance[13] to the dance schedule. The Smoke Dance,[14] which in the past was featured as a "Special," was also added to the program.[15] In order to address issues about their cultural knowledge and that of Eastern Indians, the Pequots also added a traditional Eastern Woodland exhibit to Schemitzun. This exhibit which was located directly across from the pow wow tent included a traditional Eastern Woodland village, staffed (when I attended) by Eastern Woodland people from other tribes. The staff demonstrated Eastern social dances, pottery, and other customs and traditions. Though the Pequots were demonstratively addressing issues about their Eastern Woodland traditions outside their pow wow tent, it is the issues inside of the pow wow tent that the rest of this chapter addresses.

At Schemitzun, Eastern dancers in Western categories created tensions between Western and Eastern Indians, because the Westerners felt that Easterners should dance their own dances and by not doing so, they did not know their own culture. This logic was problematic because pow wows are supposed to be a space where Native Americans share their culture through music and dance. In addition, since pow wow dances are no longer tribally specific, any Native person can dance in a dance category. Therefore, many Native people do not dance, and are not required to dance, in a category specific to their tribe or region. While the openness of dance categories fostered inclusion of all Native people in the dance circle, it has also created conflicts about the motivations of dancers who danced in categories not specific to their tribe and region; and these conflicts occurred at Schemitzun.

The judges for each dance category were dancers who either danced the same dance in another age group or danced in another category. The judges, who were often Westerners, were selected by the arena director, who was also usually from the West. Eastern Indians who performed in Western categories might "place"[16] but did not often win. I once heard a young Southern New England boy complain to his father that he knew he was the best dancer in his category, and he should have won, because he had won at other local pow wows. His father remarked that he had indeed won at local pow wows because he was judged by local people, but at events like Schemitzun he was being judge by Western Indians and if they knew his tribal affiliation they weren't going to "place" him over a Western Indian. This man's statements illuminated some of the conflicts that occurred between Easterners and Westerners at Schemitzun.

East versus West

I was afforded the opportunity to work at Schemitzun for two sequential years (2005–2006).[17] In this position, I noticed that the majority of the people in official capacities were from Western tribes. There were Pequots on the pow wow planning committee and tribal members were present in significant numbers as participants in and observers of the pow wow. Similar to other casino tribes, the Pequots could afford to have other individuals execute Schemitzun for them (Albers and Medicine 2005). Their dependence on Western Indians to fill the majority of the Schemitzun public job positions incensed many local tribal members, who complained about the lack of local representation in the pow wow's implementation.

However, one of the years I participated in the pow wow, one of the arena judges was from one of the local Wampanoag tribes. More than one person expressed excitement at his presence because it was thought that the Pequots were finally including more Eastern people in official capacities at their pow wow. However, the excitement dissipated quickly as this judge was pulled into the "Eastern versus Western Indian" dance controversy.

The Wampanoag arena director was asked to select judges for the Eastern War Dance. At the completion of the event someone filed a complaint stating that the judging of the Eastern War Dance was unfair because it was judged by Western Indians who were not familiar with Eastern dances. Since I was in the arena at the time, I was asked whether I thought the selection of judges was fair. I said I had not noticed anything irregular, and it seemed that the arena director chose a wide selection of judges. I was then pointedly asked if he chose any Eastern judges. I replied that I was not paying that close of attention to the proceedings to know.[18]

The Pequot woman who was investigating the complaint said that she was tired of all of the drama between the Western and Eastern Natives.[19] She felt that Easterners should be happy that their dances were included in Schemitzun and stop trying to "stone" one of their own. Since Schemitzun's inception there has been criticism from Western tribes about Easterners dancing in "their" categories. Although Eastern categories had been added to the dance schedule, many Eastern Indians danced in Western categories, which continued the tensions between the two groups. The Eastern judge's actions were questioned because Eastern dancers were rarely given the opportunity to judge Western dances by Western arena directors. Westerner's judging an Eastern dance competition provided the opportunity for Easterners to assert their right to judge their "own" dance competition. The tensions between Western and Eastern Indians at Schemitzun, though rarely visible to visitors, could be quite contentious and included both verbal and physical altercations.

Double Standards

This section illuminates the conflict experienced during Schemitzun when people from non-Eastern tribes started dancing in Eastern categories. During the 1600s, Native Americans from the Nipmuc, Narragansett, Pequot, and Wampanoag tribes were sold into slavery in the Caribbean (New England Indians; Adams 2003).[20] Researchers in both Southern New England and Bermuda led the efforts to reconnect the communities. As a result of these efforts, the St. David's Island Bermuda Indians held a reconnection ceremony to reunite with the New England tribes from whom their ancestors were stolen. Hence, members of Southern New England tribes visit Bermuda every two years and have a celebration/pow wow to commemorate their reconnection.

As many Bermudians migrated to the United States to live, many made it an annual tradition to attend Schemitzun in order to establish, retain, or renew contact with their Eastern Indian relatives and to become acquainted with members of other tribes. For the first few years following their reunion, the St. David's Islanders were publically recognized by their Gombey dancers. Gombey dancing is thought to be influenced by both African and Native traditions. The colorful attire worn by the dancers contains yarn, beads, and mirrors and is more reminiscent of Caribbean carnival attire rather than Native American regalia.[21]

However, after about three years of cultural exchange and interaction, men from St. David's Island started to enter the Eastern War Dance[22] competition at Schemitzun. This situation illustrated how some Western Indians may have felt about the preponderance of Eastern Indians dancing in "their" dance categories.

Many Southern Native New Englanders were upset when the Bermudians started to dance in the Eastern War Dance competition. One person commented that the presence of the Bermudians was ridiculous, because they had just recently discovered their Native connections and now thought they could dance competitively. His sentiments, which were shared by some community members, were that the Bermudians had not spent enough time in the community to participate in its cultural traditions, but this did not mean that they should not be able to eventually participate. Another person commented on one dancer's dance performance, "I was afraid to get too close to him because he might hit me with his club." This was in reference to a man who was using an Eastern War club, which some dancers use to accentuate their dance movements. Most expressed concerns that the men, who were still new to dancing, were using hatchets or clubs and might be endangering the lives of the other dancers. Though the men were concerned about dancer safety, they were also concerned about their dance being usurped by those who had only recently rediscovered their heritage.

The Bermudians' ability to participate in the Eastern War Dance demonstrated two things. First, pow wows' Pan-Indian structure allows for inclusion, that is, dancers do not have to be from a specific tribe or area to participate in a dance category, it is open to everyone. Second, because of its inclusive nature, pow wows also allow for conflict because some people are concerned that those who are not familiar with their own tribally specific customs can still participate in a Native American event, simply by learning its format, which suggests that anyone can "play Indian" (Deloria 1998). However, "playing Indian" at a pow wow did not mean that these people did not have the cultural knowledge or connections to their tribes that would make them be accepted as Indians.

The addition of the Bermudians in the Eastern War competition also comparatively illustrated the position of many Eastern Indians before they started participating in Western dances at pow wows more than 50 years ago. First, they were just trying to participate in the larger Native community through dance, some aspects of which had been lost in their specific cultures. Eastern dances still existed, but in order to participate in a Pan-Indian event like a pow wow Eastern Indians had to dance Western dances. Hence, they could not deny the Bermudians entrance into the dance competition because it would be similar to the Western Indians denying Easterners entry into Western dance categories.

Dance Motivations

The tensions between Easterners and Western Natives at Southern New England pow wows can also be understood by examining the motivations of those participating in pow wows. Although participating in a dance contest is part of Native American community building, dancing competitively at a pow wow, for some, has become a means of supporting one's self by displaying one's culture, which some might suggest is commodifying Native American culture. The fact that there is monetary gain from dancing creates questions about a dancer's motivations (Mattern 1996; Toelken 1991). Winning or placing at a pow wow can be very profitable, with first place garnering between $500 and $2,000 at some pow wows. Some Natives believe that some dancers are only motivated by monetary gain, not by the desire to participate in the Native community or to understand the significance of dancing to their culture.

Pow wow dancing does not necessitate understanding the origins or purpose of the dances being performed. At one point these dances may have been considered sacred or specific to each tribe, but some dances are no longer evaluated in this way, and anyone, Native or non-Native, can learn how to perform them. Many vendors sell instructional books and videos/DVDs on how to perform the most common Western dances. Thus, the ability of people to perform these dances does not have to be passed on from parent to child or generation to generation. They can be passed from DVD to purchaser and the meanings of the dances can be devalued by this method. The ability to learn dances from visual media instead of a person allows anyone, both Native and non-Native, to learn these dances. Native American dancing becomes less a traditional form, a form passed from Native person to Native person, but a commercialized form accessible to everyone. The ability to easily access Native American dancing traditions can also create questions about the Native ancestry of people participating in these events. In Southern New England these questions are exacerbated by the mixed heritage of tribal members and the loss of some of their cultural traditions.

Dancing at a pow wow in Southern New England can be considered an inclusive process, because dancers are rarely questioned about their tribal affiliations and because some believe that questioning others about their tribal affiliations can lead to questions about your own families' affiliations. The rules of eligibility to dance at a pow wow differ from tribe to tribe and from region to region. From my experience with Schemitzun's registration and other local pow wows, dancers are able to register without showing a tribal card. It is assumed that if you are registering for an event, you are Native American. If tribal cards were a requirement, many Native people in this area would be unable to participate because they do not possess them. Intermarriage between the tribes makes people aware that many of their relatives do not have tribal cards, but they still are Native American.

"Carding" is not a standard practice at Southern New England pow wows.[23] Thus, no one is quite sure of the tribal affiliations of the people dancing. For example, while I was sitting at the registration booth, a woman approached to register for the Eastern Blanket Dance. When she left, her dancing skills were complimented and someone asked what tribe she was from. The response was

"I think she is White, with no tribal affiliation, but she sure can dance." The ease in which dancers can register at pow wows like Schemitzun does not go unnoticed by dancers. Once a dancer is registered and receives a number for categorization, they can win a prize. Thus, many understand that anyone, including non-Natives, can find their way into the dancing circle by acquiring the skills to perform the dances, which suggests anyone can participate in these dances. This blurs the line between who is and who is not Indian during these events and further complicates the question about the authenticity of the Native Americans in this area.

I questioned a few pow wow registrars about how often people with no tribal affiliations entered events. I was informed that it was not a frequent occurrence. There were deterrents, such as the price of the regalia people were required to wear. In addition, most people were not willing to face the embarrassment if their tribal connections were questioned. In one instance when a dancer's tribal affiliation was questioned by another dancer in her category at Schemitzun, the situation was handled by the dance registrars. Registrars are local tribal people, usually from the host tribe, and they monitor those entering the dance competitions. They discretely inquired with elders in this woman's tribe and other members of her community in order to verify her tribal affiliation.

During my time in Southern New England, "carding" was suggested at different pow wow planning committee meetings to curb constant fighting between Narragansett and Shinnecock youth at pow wows. In 2005, the local police departments were forced to tear gas the youths in order to stop the fighting at Schemitzun. The fights would occur during the sequential weekends of the Narragansett, Mohegan, Pequot, and Shinnecock pow wows. The fighting has led to serious injuries including the disfigurement of one young woman. It was thought that carding would help monitor the number of people attending the pow wow from different tribes. The carding suggestion was met with resistance since many Native people in the area did not have tribal cards because they were not from federally recognized tribes or were not on their tribal roll. At one tribe's pow wow planning committee meeting, one prominent member of the Native community argued against the motion saying she would not be allowed to participate in the pow wows because she did not have a tribal card, although it was widely known that her family was Indian.

This is another situation in which pow wows can force Native Americans in the area to confront the difficulties in recognizing themselves and others as Indians. Tribal cards, which can be used to validate one's Native identity, are not accessible to all in this region since some tribes have not been federally recognized. Local pow wows allow Southern New England Native Americans to interact and dance with both local tribal members and those from other tribes, without proof of Native American identity or tribal affiliation. Outside of Southern New England, other pow wows might require proof of tribal membership in order for them to participate.

"Doesn't She Really Look Like an Indian?"

One of the major areas of contention between Western and Eastern Indians at pow wows was the varying appearance of Native Southern New Englanders. The presence of large numbers of Western Indians at Eastern pow wows inevitably led to comparisons between Eastern and Western people. One of the most frequent comparisons was that of physical appearance. Native Americans in Southern New England were aware that intermarriage with other groups has led to variations in their culture, history, and physical appearance. However, instead of explaining these phenomena, some tried to authenticate themselves as Native Americans by denoting that there were Native people in Southern New England who resembled Western Indians.

In order to dispel or refute claims that little or no Native American ancestry or culture remained in Southern New England, some Native Americans who live in this area have utilized real or imagined kinship ties to associate themselves with Eastern Natives who resembled Western Indians. This approach was often used by people who did not resemble the Native American stereotype, of the brown skinned, high cheek boned, and black haired individual. My interviews contain numerous accounts of people being stopped during Schemitzun and being called cousin by people they did not know, especially if the interviewee resembled Western Indians. An interviewee recalled that she was walking by the food booths at Schemitzun when she was stopped by someone she barely knew and was introduced as their cousin. Another woman mentioned that at Schemitzun a family member introduced her to a friend and said, "Now doesn't she really look like an Indian?"

Appearance or one's "face"[24] is a very important aspect of an individual's persona in Native Southern New England. A person's Native identity is not questioned by non-Natives or other Natives if they "look" Native American. However, many Southern Native New Englanders do not "look" Native American, but are enrolled members of state or federally recognized tribes. Many have tribal cards which validate their Native status, but the significance placed on Native appearance impacts whether their claims to be Native American are given credence by other Indians and non-Indians.

In Southern New England family disputes have occurred between those who "look Indian" and those who do not. These family conflicts, though divisive, do not change a person's membership in their tribe or the Native community. However, during large pow wows like Schemitzun the conflicts about identity were exacerbated when these communities shared the stage with Western Indians who were the prototype for the stereotype of how Native Americans should appear. Family, community, and tribal conceptions of Native American identity in this area, which are in constant flux, were pushed to their limits by challenges to Native identity based on appearance. The pressure to look Indian in this area created and furthered disputes amongst families, tribal members, and outsiders who felt that one had to look Indian in order to be Indian.

As a pow wow, Schemitzun enabled Western Indians and the Indians of Southern New England to interact for four days out of the year, uniting groups that may have not interacted previously due to distance. This unification was not without disputes. Schemitzun was often a venue in which the authenticity of local tribes and Native people was questioned. Schemitzun's emphasis on Western Indian culture gave the perception that there was little of Eastern Native culture remaining in the region. By emphasizing turquoise and teepees over and wampum and wetus some local Indians and some of their Western counterparts questioned whether or not the Pequots were aware of their Eastern Woodland culture. Some Western Indians also believed that the perceived lack of cultural awareness on the Pequots' part was reflective of all people in Southern New England. Hence, at Schemitzun, conflicts between Eastern Indians and Western Indians about the authenticity of Eastern Indians as Native people constantly occurred.

Conclusion

Since pow wows emphasize Native American culture and identity, not tribally specific identity, they force people to confront issues of race, identity, and authenticity in Southern New England. When Southern New England was host to three of the largest pow wows in the United States, Schemitzun, Mohegan Wigwam, and Shinnecock, Native communities, both Eastern and Western Indians, came together to celebrate their Native identity. These pow wows were access points into the Native community that illustrated the tension about who was and who was not Native American and how these determinations were made.

Pow wows can blur the distinctiveness between individual tribes and create a space for those Native individuals and tribes whose access to the Native American community has been limited physically, socially, and politically. In Southern New England, pow wows are venues in which both race and cultural knowledge become factors in determining a person's access to both their local Native community and the larger Native American community. While pow wows can blur the lines of a tribe's cultural specificity, they also reinforce the belief that some Native cultural knowledge and traditions, like dance, are static; and if these traditions are not adhered to they can create questions about your authenticity as a Native American.

Questions about the ancestry, culture, physical appearance, and the authenticity of Native Southern New Englanders were prevalent when Schemitzun, Mohegan Wigwam, and Shinnecock drew large numbers of Western Indian participants. Since local tribes had to contend with other Natives who questioned their authenticity at these pow wows, they hampered the unity of these communities. Central to this divisiveness was the Pequots' Western Indian-oriented pow wow, Schemitzun.

Schemitzun's original intent—to unite the Southern New England community with Western Native communities, created more dissent than unity in Southern New England. Although many were impressed by Schemitzun's splendor and gallantry, many others were not. The tribe's local critics, which included public officials and a few local tribal members, argued that the Pequots' money allowed them to buy an "authentic" identity, one based on Western Indian stereotypes. Schemitzun's dependence on Western Indian cultural values garnered contempt from some Westerners who believed that all Native people in Southern New England had lost their culture. Some Southern New England tribes resented being associated with the Pequots and did not want Westerners and non-Indians to believe that the Pequots, their knowledge and lifestyle, were representative of all Native people in Southern New England. The conflict about Native American identity has created resentment between some Southern Native New Englanders and cultural misunderstandings between some Western and Eastern Natives.

Pow wows exacerbated tensions about how different the tribes of Southern New England were from their Western counterparts. Pow wows also forced these tribes to confront ideas about their authenticity as Native Americans. Their cultural knowledge and ancestry, which for many individuals are both private and subjective matters, were challenged by outsiders unfamiliar with their history. Conflicts that existed before events like Schemitzun, between families, friends, and tribal members about what it means to be Native American, were relived every summer and were on display for people from outside of Native New England to observe.

Notes

1 Southern New England here refers to Connecticut, Massachusetts, and Rhode Island.
2 Questions about whether or not Native Americans in Southern New England are really Indians.
3 Blackness here equates to African ancestry, phenotype, and culture.
4 The Narragansett August Meeting/Green Corn Thanksgiving, which is reported to be over three hundred years old, is the first weekend in August.
5 The Mashantucket Pequots or the Western Pequots, will be referred to as the Pequots in the chapter. There is also the tribe known as the Eastern Pequots.
6 Originally prize amounts were $5,000 for first place, and in 2009 when the Pequot canceled the larger Schemitzun and scaled back its size and prize money this dramatically decreased the participation of Western tribes.
7 This is true of both the larger and smaller Schemitzun.
8 By hosting a pow wow, the Pequots demonstrated to other Native Americans and non-Natives that as a federally recognized wealthy tribe, as demonstrated by their casino, they could host a large Native American cultural event.
9 That is Native Americans who had stereotypic Native American features such as brown skin and long, straight, dark hair.
10 The Narragansett August meeting occurs the first weekend in August, making it a part of the New England pow wow calendar.
11 This section has been adapted from my master's thesis "They Don't Look Like Indians to Me: (Mis)Conceptions of the Mashantucket Pequot of Connecticut."
12 The Eastern Blanket Dance was the first Eastern dance to become a part of Schemitzun about four years after it started.
13 The Eastern War Dance, formally known as the Eastern Straight Dance, is thought to have originated with the Haudenosaunees.
14 The Smoke Dance is a fast stepped dance usually performed by the Haudenosaunees.

15 The "Special" category is used for dances that are not featured yearly or as a fundraiser for certain causes.
16 By place I mean that although they do not win, they finish in 2nd, 3rd, or 4th position.
17 In 2013 and 2014 I also worked at the smaller Schemitzun.
18 I was obviously paying close enough attention to the proceedings to document them, but wanted to stay out of the conflict.
19 Because of the rampant number of grievances received at Schemitzun, the Pequots threatened to charge $100 for filing a complaint.
20 http://freepages.genealogy.rootsweb.ancestry.com/~massasoit/bermuda.htm. (This page no longer exists).
21 Gombey costumes include masks, are brightly colored, and contain glitter and yarn. They are similar to outfits worn at Brazilian or Caribbean carnivals. Native American regalia, which can be brightly colored, often includes natural elements such as buckskin, animal feathers, bones, and teeth.
22 The Eastern War Dance, whose previous name was the Eastern Straight Dance, originated from the Calumet Dance. The Calumet Dance was a sacred dance performed by Eastern men during the pipe ceremony, where Eastern men's bodies represented the stem of the pipe and their heads, the bowl.
23 However, in recent years it has become more common.
24 I use the word face to represent physical appearance.

References

Adams, Jim. 2003. "Gombey Dancers Mark Reunion." *Indian Country Today* (16): B1.
Adams, Jim. 2002. "Pequots Working Diplomatic Angles, Invite UN Group to Schemitzun 2002." *Indian Country Today*. Available at: http://www.indiancountrytoday.com/archive/28220479.html, accessed October 25, 2010.
Albers, Patricia C., and Beatrice Medicine. 2005. "Some Reflections on nearly Forty Years on the Northern Plains Powwow Circuit." In *Powwow*. Clyde Ellis, Luke E. Lassiter and Gary H. Dunham, eds. pp. 26–45. Lincoln: University of Nebraska Press.
Arndt, Grant. 2016. *Ho-Chunk Powwows and the Politics of Tradition*. Lincoln: The University of Nebraska Press.
Arndt, Grant. 2004. No Middle Ground: Ho-Chunk Powwows and the Production of SocialSpace in Native Wisconsin. Ph.D. dissertation, The University of Chicago.
Browner, Tara. 2002. *Heartbeat of the People: Music and Dance of the Northern Pow-Wow* Urbana: University of Illinois Press.
Cook, Samuel R., John L. Johns, and Karenne Wood. 2005. "The Monacan Nation Powwow: Symbols of Indigenous Survival and Resistance in the Tobacco Row Mountains." In *Powwow*. Clyde Ellis, Luke E. Lassiter and Gary H. Dunham, eds. pp. 201–223. Lincoln: University of Nebraska Press.
Deloria, Philip Joseph. 1998. *Playing Indian*. New Haven, CT: Yale University Press.
Ellis, Clyde. 2005. "The Sound of the Drum Will Revive Them and Make Them Happy." In *Powwow*. Clyde Ellis, Luke E. Lassiter and Gary H. Dunham, eds. pp. 3–25. Lincoln: University of Nebraska Press.
Ellis, Clyde. 2003. *A Dancing People: Powwow Culture on the Southern Plains*. Lawrence: University Press of Kansas.
Ellis, Clyde, and Luke E. Lassiter. 2005. "Introduction." In *Powwow*. Clyde Ellis, Luke E. Lassiter and Gary H. Dunham, eds. pp. vii–xv. Lincoln: University of Nebraska Press.
Fromson, Brett Duval. 2003. *Hitting the Jackpot: The Inside Story of the Richest Indian Tribe in History*. 1st ed. New York: Atlantic Monthly Press.

Gilley, Brian Joseph. 2005. "Two-Spirit Powwows and the Search for Social Acceptance in Indian Country." In *Powwow*. Clyde Ellis, Luke E. Lassiter and Gary H. Dunham, eds. pp. 224–240. Lincoln: University of Nebraska Press.

Goertzen, Chris. 2005. "Purposes of North Carolina Powwows." In *Powwow*. Clyde Ellis, Luke E. Lassiter and Gary H. Dunham, eds. pp. 275–302. Lincoln: University of Nebraska Press.

Goertzen, Chris. 2001. "Powwows and Identity on the Piedmont and Coastal Plains of North Carolina." *Ethnomusicology* 45(1): 58–88.

Hatoum, Rainer. 1999. The "(INTERTRIBAL) POWWOW" AS A "CULTURAL PHENOMENON": A Discussion of the Term "Culture." *European Review of Native American Studies* 13(1): 47–49.

Mattern, Mark. 1996. "The Powwow as a Public Arena for Negotiating Unity and Diversity in American Indian Life." *American Indian Culture and Research Journal* 20(4): 183–201.

McMullen, Ann. 1996. "Soapbox Discourse: Tribal Historiography, Indian-White Relations, and Southeastern New England Powwows." *The Public Historian* 18(4, Representing Native American History): 53–74.

New England Indians – Bermuda/Pequot Reconnection Festival. 2002. n.d. Electronic document, http://freepages.genealogy.rootsweb.ancestry.com/~massasoit/bermuda.htm, accessed 2006.

Oxford English Dictionary, s.v. "Powwow," accessed 2006, http://dictionary.oed.com.

Povinelli, Elizabeth A. 2002. *The Cunning of Recognition: Indigenous Alterities and the Making of Australian Multiculturalism*. Durham, NC: Duke University Press.

Toelken, Barre. 1991. "Ethnic Selection and Intensification in the Native American Powwow." In *Creative Ethnicity: Symbols and Strategies of Contemporary Ethnic Life*. Stephen Stern and John Allan Cicala, eds. pp. 137–156. Logan: Utah State University Press.

Watchman, Renae. 2005. "Powwow Overseas: The German Experience." In *Powwow*. Clyde Ellis, Luke E. Lassiter and Gary H. Dunham, eds. pp. 241–257. Lincoln: University of Nebraska Press.

Witthoft, John. 1949. *Green Corn Ceremonialism in the Eastern Woodlands*. Vol. no. 13. Ann Arbor: University of Michigan Press.

Young, Gloria Alese. 1981. "Powwow Power: Perspectives on Historic and Contemporary Intertribalism." Ph.D. dissertation, Indiana University.

PART III
Prospects for Future Research

6

AFRICAN AND NATIVE AMERICAN CONTACT IN MEXICO, CENTRAL, AND SOUTH AMERICA

Prospects for Twenty-First Century Research

Robert Keith Collins

> In Mexico and Central America, the negro has amalgamated not only with the whites, but with the indigenous population of the country in such a measure, that he is not anything like as distinct a people as in the United States. The same process of miscegenation has served to confuse the African blood in all the tropical regions of South America.
>
> *(Shaler 1890: 671)*

Several explanations of the dynamics of contact between Africans and Native Americans in Mexico, Central, and South America can be found in the anthropological, historical, and social scientific literature. In the quote above, Shaler (1890) reminds us that interactions and intermarriage between Africans and Native Americans were extensive enough that African ancestry can be found in people living throughout the tropical regions of South America. While explanatory gaps exist in the literature for countries not yet researched, there are several examples that reveal the nature and source of these interactions. As in the United States, African and Native American contact must be considered as part of the larger processes of European and Native American contact and African enslavement and displacement to the Western Hemisphere.

Within anthropology, what could be called historical anthropological interest in these interactions lies in paleontologist and geologist N.S. Schaler's (1890) examination of "The African Element in the America." Relevant components of this broad analysis were exploration of the state of African Americans and interactions with Native Americans. Although the interactions are discussed in terms of comingling of blood, Shaler's comparative analysis of variation among African descended peoples in North, Central, and South American led him to the concluding fact that,

> We are even more at a loss to ascertain the present number of negroes in these continents: in fact, this point is probably indeterminable, for the reason that the African blood has commingled with that of the European and the aborigines in an incalculable manner.
>
> *(Schaler 1890: 666)*

Works that followed examined the nature of these interactions by country and their relevance to the larger national population. Although the focus taken was on locations within Mexico and nations within Central and South America with the largest imported African slave populations, they contain detailed discussions of the impact that interactions between Africans and Indigenous populations had on the population composition (Belt; Reuter; Gibbons; Clemenceau).

Laurence Foster (1978) provided one of the most comprehensive summaries of works on this impact by country and the collective names used in reference to the populations. For example, in Guatemala, populations comprising African and Native American mixtures were often referred to as Ladinos and formed a significant part of the population. In Mexico, African descended individuals could be found among the Indigenous populations (Beltran 1984: 1–5). This was also true in Panama; however, the largest population in the Caribbean that was reflective of this mixture was in Cuba. According to Foster's research, "...there are a considerable number of persons who are mixed with Indians, Negro, and Spanish blood" (Foster 1978: 9).

Works revealed that in Nicaragua, individuals of blended African and Indigenous ancestry comprised the majority of the population, and in Ecuador, individuals of this blended ancestry were referred to as Zambos and formed a significant majority of the total population. In Venezuela and Paraguay, individuals of blended African and Native American ancestry could be found among a small portion of the populations. Agassiz and Agassiz (1868) noted in Brazil, as in the United States, Africans were enslaved by both Europeans and Native Americans. Through African and Native American interactions, voluntary and involuntary, in servitude and in the interior of Brazil, "a distinct physical type was formed by the union of Negro and Indian." The impact of the institution of slavery on Africans lent to the creation of a population of blended African, Native American, and European ancestry that formed approximately one-third of the nation's population (Agassiz and Agassiz 1868: 292; Foster 1978: 10).

More contemporary work by Joseph Palacio (1992) shed light on the origins of this blended ancestry and its relationship to Garifuna identity in "The Sojourn Toward Self Discovery Among Caribbean Indigenous Peoples." According to Palacio, the Garifuna or Black Carib as referred to by early English "were formed by the intermixture of maroon African slaves with Carib Indians in St. Vincent" (Palacio 1992: 61). This diasporic population of St. Vincent live throughout the Caribbean, with the largest populations in Belize and Honduras. Two of the largest diasporic populations now reside in Los Angeles and New York in the United States (Palacio 2009).

Outside of anthropology, historians created analytical frameworks that aided in the explanation and examination of the social and cultural elements of African and Native American interactions (McDonald 1998: 21–22). In 1946, Frank Tannenbaum's (1992) history of the relationship between "Slave and Citizen" comparatively illuminated how social role acquisition shaped the interactions between Africans and Native Americas in the Western Hemisphere. Through this framework an important element examined was the profitability of slavery for both Europeans and Native Americans, which enabled intermixture between African and Native Americans (Tannenbaum 1992: 1–5; Collins 2017: 1–3; 2021).

Tannenbaum's analysis further revealed how individuals of blended African and Native American ancestry were also the result of Africans escaping into the interior of Brazil and occasionally enslaved Indigenous peoples. The relationships formed created common African and Indigenous cultural lifeways that distinguished those of blended ancestry from other populations in Brazil. Magnus Morner (1969) examined the experiences of the children of Africans and Native Americans as a component of the larger history of "Race Mixture in the History of Latin America" (1969). Morner also documented how in the 1640s scholars of Spanish American law, such as Juan de Solórzano, actively compared mestizos with and against mulattoes and Zambos to codify which mixture was the most socially acceptable (Morner 1969: 43; Beltran 1982: 1–2). Although work has been done documenting the history of the various race mixtures that occurred between populations, what these populations experienced and what their descendants say today remain in need of academic attention (Collins 2021: 1–3).

The prospects for researching African-Native Americans in the history of Latin America presented here developed out of these previously discussed works, the richness of their references, and represent an endeavor to fill explanatory gaps in the literature. In order to enhance the relevance of these prospects, the works were reviewed for their ability to be applied to expand the anthropological record and the various fields engaged in the explanation of African and Native American contact. In this brief review, themes in the literature of shared kinship, collective definition of new humans of blended African and Native American ancestry, and competition between mestizos, mulattoes, and Zambos allow future researchers to develop original works that challenge, revisit, and/or revitalize previous assumptions made from primary sources in the anthropological and historical records. In a similar vein, ethnographic fieldwork can be conducted that sheds light on how individuals experience being African-Native American and belonging within Latin American nations (Greiffenstern and Raab 1993: 1–3; Collins 2021: 1–5).

Specifying Interactions

To understand the formulation of African-Native American identities in Latin America, it is necessary to clarify a few collective names used throughout the Western Hemisphere to index the population. For the purposes of this discussion, a set of terms are defined in association with the social roles individuals acquired (Thornton and Nardi 1975: 870–872). There are several possible sources of these terms. First, they may be general notions applied to populations of blended African-Native American ancestry to index them as African descendants, despite Native American parentage or ancestry. This means that these are social recognition practices and represent common sense racial ways of indexing people within society during a certain time period. This common sense can be derived from legal definition or peoples' expectations and social attitudes. Second, these terms may also represent the social role or social condition of individuals to whom they are ascribed. For example, Morner's (1969) research revealed that the term "Mestizo" in the common Mexican parlance of the 1600s was synonymous with illegitimate (Morner 1969: 42–43). The same phenomenon could be seen with the term Negro being synonymous with being a slave during the same time period. Despite term usage, two states of being may be distinguished. People identifying in accordance with racial recognition practices in public and people identifying with culture, family, and kin in private. These formulations often change from public to private use depending upon expectations of acceptance and rejection.

These collective terms for African-Native Americans include but are not limited to Lobo (used in Mexico and throughout eighteenth-century New Spain), Negro, Zambaigo (children of an African-Native American and a Native American), Sambo de Indio (used in Peru to describe a child of an African and a Native American), and Zambo. It is important to note that the latter term was also used in much of the Western Hemisphere to describe African-Native Americans; however, in Peru, the term described the children of an African and mulatto or individuals of blended Spanish and African parentage (Morner 1969: 57–59; Forbes 1993:1–5). Therefore, these terms require awareness of the context-dependent, implicit, and explicit expectations of identity each term represents. These expectations may also not have had consensus depending upon people's racial attitudes or if individuals affiliated or were raised with one parent or culture, over the other, which make contemporary ethnographic investigations of descendant lived experiences so important. Such ethnographies would fill the explanatory gap of how these terms change over time and the relevance they hold for contemporary African-Native American understandings of self (Csordas 1990: 1–2, 1997: 1–5; Collins 2021: 1–2).

Understanding African-Native Americans in Latin America

A growing interest in the study of African and Native American contact in Mexico, Central, and South America has developed among anthropologists, Ethnic Studies scholars, historians, and social scientists in the twenty-first century. Following in the tradition of Morner (1969), the basic approach has been to examine the history of African presence among Indigenous populations, the extent of mixture between Africans and Native Americans, and the racial terminology used to describe them. Typically, this approach lends to the review of primary sources about the nature of interactions between African and Native American from the historical record. While the historical record does not fully describe all aspects of these interactions, they usually offer a thorough snapshot of African-Native American presence and variations in Mestizo, Indigenous, and Spaniard attitude toward individuals with this parentage (Zapf 1999: 302–305).

My current research interest in African and Native American contact and African-Native Americans in Latin America came from fieldwork findings made, and works reviewed, while a member of the curatorial team for the Smithsonian's traveling banner exhibit, "IndiVisible: African-Native American Lives in the Americas." Taking a person-centered ethnographic approach to understanding Garifuna lived experiences in South Central Los Angeles, CA, an approach which seeks to get as close as possible to first-person experience within culture, revealed that the shared African and Native American cultural and linguistic or "Island Arawak" elements of being Garifuna were often ignored, not only by conventional racial recognition practices but historical as well (Collins 2009, 2021; Hollan 1997: 1–2; Palacio 2009). These findings were similar to those found by Barreiro (2009) in his research among African descended Taino and McFarren (2009) in his research among Afro-Aymara in Bolivia that contributes to Tayac's (2009) edited volume that accompanied the exhibit. African-Native Americans seemed to be indexed by race, which left their cultural practices illusive, unless historians recorded their cultural affiliations or, for example, as in Mexico, noted them as 'hijos del pueblo," or children of the town or village (Kanter 2006: 171).

According to Kanter, and given the diversity of African descended individuals living in Indigenous Mexican towns and villages (i.e., Africans, Afro-Mexicans, and African-Native American), "The acceptance of Afro-Mexicans in Indian pueblos depended on a complex mix of biological and social factors. Birthplace and family ties were crucial. An Afro-Mexican born in the pueblo where he or she resided earned community acceptance" (Kanter 2006: 170). Kanter's research also revealed that, "While kinship ties allowed Afro-Mexicans to enter Indian villages, they fared best if they followed village rules: living settled lives, serving the *republica* (village government) or church, and obeying Indian authorities. Royal authorities seem to ignore segregation laws if Afro-Mexicans living in Indian villages paid tribute" (Kanter 2006: 170).

Although non-Native individuals could file complaints seeking to enforce colonial segregation laws, they were seldom enforced by authorities.

Barreiro's (2009) fieldwork among the Taino of Puerto Rico contributed greatly to understandings of the perennial need of fieldwork with African-Native Americans and how anti-African and anti-Black racial attitudes within a society could undermine social knowledge of the dynamics of cultural interactions that occurred historically between Africans and Native Americans. Taking the intersections of Taino and African populations as the central focus of analysis, Barreiro illustrated the tensions between marginalized Taino Indigenous communities and new popular movements by "neo-Tainos" to claim Taino identity, which Afro-Taino are caught between and further marginalized. For some, the monolithic use of Taino identity seems to erase the African ancestry of many and, for others, Taino is seen as replacing mestizaje (Barreiro 2009: 39).

Interviews with Taino leaders revealed a more inclusive attitude toward African ancestry: an attitude that takes African ancestry as a component of being Taino. For example, one leader told Barreiro,

> I am Indian, natural from Boriken. The African culture, the African blood, also runs in my veins. In fact, being Taino does not diminish my pride of the African in me... So I am proud to have African blood. I am Taino. Yet, in saying so, I do not deny, how could I, the fact of my African blood.
> *(Barreiro 2009: 41)*

Another leader reminded Barreiro (2009) that,

> There is mestizaje, with African, with Español. Racially, if you accept the term, we are a blended people. But Taino is not about race. It is about culture. Taino and African were slaves together and together fought against the colony. In our movement there is not racism; there is not a wish to deny the black nor the white in us or outside us. We come from our own member in our families, not from books... I identify with my culture, not with a race.
> *(Barreiro 2009: 41)*

Barreiro's respondents provide insight into the meaning-making factors behind their formulations of Taino identity and the integral role that African ancestry has played.

McFarren's (2009) fieldwork in Dorado Chico, Bolivia, illuminated how contemporary Afro-Bolivian cultural revitalization movements contained elements of their own cultural traditions, but also, especially for those from the Bolivian highlands, shared Aymara cultural traditions were also practiced. In Dorado Chico, where Afro-Bolivians and Aymara live together, celebrations of their patron saint San Benito is a shared cultural event. This shared culture between Afro-Bolivian and Aymara can also be seen in the everyday life. McFarren captured community sentiments about this shared culture during an interview with an Afro-Bolivian community leader, "We can no longer talk about 'cultural purity,' because a cultural syncretism is what we actually have..." (McFarren 2009: 199). An example of this lived syncretism captured by McFarren's work can be seen in the clothing of Afro-Bolivian women. "Afro-Bolivian women wear the same dress and braid their hair in the same style as the Aymaras; some even speak Aymara" (McFarren 2009: 199).

Findings from McFarren's fieldwork reminds us that external appearances in shared culture can be both revealing and deceiving. Without insight into the meaning-making factors of being Afro-Bolivian, shared Aymara cultural elements would remain overshadowed by expectations associated with racial categorization. Such expectations would also overshadow the shared history of Afro-Bolivians and Aymara that caused them to continue living with one another. According to McFarren (2009), "Although slavery was abolished in 1851, it was not until the 1952 revolution, followed by the passing of the Agrarian Reform Law, that Afro-Bolivians and indigenous peoples were freed from indentured servitude and allowed to be landowners" (McFarren 2009: 197). Shared histories of slavery and resistance to oppression in the formulation of African-Native American identities resonated in the narratives of many respondents whose lives informed the exhibit; however, while the identities of being African-Native Americans or Native American were evident, it was among the Garifuna that its "IndiVisible" nature could be seen.

Historically recognized as Black Carib or Negro, the Garifuna of Los Angeles, CA, represented a variety of cultural mixtures indelibly linked to their diasporic past and present. Not only were they African and Native American from St. Vincent, the mixture and island of their origins, but also reflected the Belizean, Honduran, Mayan, and Afro-Latin populations that they intermarried with in diaspora, as well as African American populations of the United States. Despite the national and racial diversity they embody, Garifuna culture and language are kept central by many in everyday life and all are encouraged to avoid "*gudémei lidan samínü*" (short-sightedness). According to Joseph O. Palacio, Sr.,

> The Garifuna people have been migrating to cities such as New York, Boston, Chicago, Los Angeles, and New Orleans since the early 1900s. Among the approximately 300,000 Garifuna in Central America, most have at least one close relative from Belize, Guatemala, Honduras, or Nicaragua living in the United States.
>
> *(Palacio 2009: 91)*

This diversity was evident during my fieldwork in Los Angeles, CA.

During interviews with Garifuna American Heritage Foundation United community members, it became evident that the short-sightedness young Garifuna were encourage to avoid was part of an age-old struggle between two cultures, between being African American or Afro-Latino and being Garifuna, that often led to the neglect of Garifuna culture due to social pressure. Respondents that informed this discussion were interviewed during the summer of 2008. Respondents live in both single and extended family households and gather regularly for ceremonies like the Hudutu or Hudutu Baruru, "The Feast of Slumber," which comprise religious rites and rites of passage. The pressure from family to maintain Garifuna culture, and African American and Latin American social peers to conform, often led to some young Garifuna being recognized by peers as different. According to Palacio (2009), it is important to remember that this difference has a history and this difference that Garifuna embody has a patterning of culture,

> ...developed through the mixing of Indians and blacks on St. Vincent. The blending of Arawak and Caribs is one of the many interesting mixtures in the history of the Garifuna people, and highlights the fact that the mixing of people had been happening long before Africans and the Garifuna ever came into contact with each other. Originating from two Amazonian forest peoples in present-day Venezuela, the Arawaks and Caribs remained distinct in language, belief systems, and material cultures as they moved into the Caribbean. The Arawaks are Taino people who still live today on the Greater Antilles islands of Cuba, Jamaica, Hispanola, and Puerto Rico. They passed their language to their descendants, some of whom became the Garifuna.
> *(Palacio 2009: 93–94)*

Palacio reminds us that more research is need into the alliances and blending of cultures between the Arawak and Carib that created the Yellow Caribs of the eastern Caribbean and were the immediate ancestors of the Garifuna. In many everyday Garifuna lives, like their ancestors, the challenge is to maintain identity while adapting and living as African American and/or Afro-Latino, or Latino depending upon appearance, is a way of life. Interviews with members of the Garifuna community shed light on the nature of the challenge. Originally from Guatemala, Ms. Norales pointed out that, "For many years, people wanted us to be invisible. They wanted us to just blend in and be Black American, be African American, don't be who you are." Despite the pressure of conformity, as Palacio reminds us, the strength behind Garifuna endurance has come from an ability to adapt to changing cultural and national surroundings. According to Ms. Norales, this adaptation enabled the Garifuna to,

> ...still practice our spirituality, the same way our ancestors did. We still prepare our food the same way our ancestors did. Nobody was able to take that away from us. Nobody. As hard as they tried, they could not take that away from us.

During an interview with the Mr. Alvez, a community member and renowned Garifuna drummer, he recalled his experiences with pressure to conform while a student in Honduras.

> I was going to college in Honduras and the principal, he said to me,You are the only Black person that is speaking this language. Look at all of your Garinagu people. They speak Spanish. And, ironically, you are the most eloquent Spanish speaker of them all; however, you insist speaking this language of yours. Why? I asked him, teacher, you really want me to answer that question? Yes, yes. he said. You won't expel me? No, he said.

Look at you. You are Spanish. Um, you are put in an ethnic bracket as a Mestizo. That means mixed, right? He looked at me and shook his head. He asked, what do you mean by that? Well, you are not a Spaniard. You are no longer an Indian. I am a Garifuna. I am Black. Nobody can change this or mistake me for being something else or call me Mestizo. He said, get back to class! Since then, I have a strong feeling about ... the way of Garinagu, the way of our ancestry...

Implications and Conclusion

Given the literature reviewed on the history of African and Native American contact in Latin America and the accounts of African-Native American lived experiences that reflect this history, what implications do they hold for research? One point learned from these investigations is that if ethnographic and historical research is slanted toward race and race mixture, then the culture, cultural diversity, and cultural maintenance African-Native Americans in Latin America embody may be overlooked; however, this does not mean that a historical account of African and Native American contact, that only focuses on primary sources noting the blended ancestry of children from these dynamic contacts, will not correspond with the contemporary cultural concerns of descendants. Researching African and Native American contact in Latin America can illuminate the intersections of African and Native American cultures and kinship ties and the many African experiences, slave and free, and Native American experiences, slave and sovereign, that shaped being and belonging for their many descendants. Individuals today continue to assert shared cultural identities formed out of a racial past.

The general discussion of this chapter is that studying African and Native Americans contact in Latin America enables an understanding of this contact as part of a hemispheric phenomenon. The goal of this discussion is to revitalize interest in the historical research that has inspired contemporary investigations of the phenomenon and the lived experiences that informed academic understanding. Challenging racial reductionism has been an inherent component of the study of African and Native American contact and characteristic of the analyses that have shaped this incredible aspect of cultural change in North, Central, and South America. Discovering new frontiers in the study of African-Native Americans in Latin America requires an interrogation of how and why Afro-Latin cultures and peoples have been marginalized from mestizaje and the role this marginalization played in overshadowing Native American ancestry among African descended populations (Hallowell 1963: 1–4).

The anthropological and historical foundations upon which this discussion is built bring attention to the need for greater theoretical investigation – and ethnographic fieldwork – into how the social use of racial terminology, in relationship to social condition and social roles, lent to the erasure of social knowledge around the tribal-specific heritages African-Native Americans embodied in the past and their descendants continue to embody in the present. Conscious and unconscious social denial and rejection of African ancestry should no longer be a barrier to furthering academic understanding of the integrated presence that African-Native Americans had in Latin America (Sapir 1929). Such a barrier is indicative of the attitudes and practices surrounding African ancestry in various countries and is important for academic investigation for three reasons. One, this barrier suggests a casual and uncontested link between racial attitudes and classification terminology and African-Native American self-understandings, without specifying the extent to which African-Native American populations found these terms salient in their identities. Enabling such a barrier perpetuates the myth that what a society thinks about a marginalized people within its population is who these people are. Two, researching this barrier can reveal the extent to which terms indexing African and Native American parentage and ancestry were internalized by populations. Revitalization movements, like those of the Taino, and cultural maintenance efforts by those of the Garifuna, suggest that this is not always the case. There is much more to learn and new formulations of African-Native American identities from the descendants of a people who have maintained an identity over time, despite marginalization. Three, different individuals accept, reject, and internalize racial identities in unique ways. Variation in individual internalization of racial identities has seldom been examined and renders the cultural and ancestral diversity of those classified as Lobo, Sambo de Indio, and Zambo illusive. To understand the dynamics of African and Native American contact in Latin America requires new examinations of the anthropological and historical records. The works presented in this discussion provide a solid foundation upon which to begin.

Works Cited

Agassiz, Elizabeth Cabot Cary, and Louis Agassiz. 1868. *A Journey in Brazil*. Brazil: Ticknor and Fields.

Aguirre Beltrán, Gonzalo. 1982 [1957]. *El proceso de aculturación*. 1. ed. en Ediciones de la Casa Chata. México: Centro de Investigaciones y Estudios Superiores en Antropología Social.

———. *La población negra de México : estudio etnohistórico*. 1984. 2a. ed. México: FCE.

Barreiro, Jose. "Taino-African Intersection: Elite Constructs and Resurgent Identities." In *IndiVisible: African-Native American Lives in the Americas*. Ed. Gabrielle Tayac (Washington, DC: Smithsonian Books, 2009), 35–42.

Collins, Robert Keith. "What Is a Black Indian? Misplaced Expectations and Lived Realities." In *IndiVisible: African-Native American Lives in the Americas*. Ed. Gabriella Tayac (Washington, DC: Smithsonian Books, 2009), 183–196.

———. *African and Native American Contact in the U.S.: Anthropological and Historical Perspectives*. San Diego, CA: Cognella Academic Publishing, 2017.

———. "Toward an Inter-American Study of African Transculturalization in Native America." In *Colonialism, Coloniality, and Decolonization in the Americas*. Eds. Josef Raab and Alexia Schemien (Tempe, AZ: Wissenschaftlicher Verlag Trier/Bilingual Press, 2021), 91–102.

Csordas, Thomas J. 1990. "The 1988 Stirling Award Essay: Embodiment as a Paradigm for Anthropology." *Ethos (Berkeley, Calif.)* 18 (1): 5.
———. 1997. *The Sacred Self: A Cultural Phenomenology of Charismatic Healing.* Berkeley, CA: University of California Press.
Forbes, Jack D. *Africans and Native Americans: The Language of Race and the Evolution of Red-Black Peoples.* Urbana-Champaign: U of Illinois P, 1993.
Foster, Laurence. *Negro-Indian Relations in the Southeast.* New York: AMS Press, 1978.
Greiffenstern, Alexander, and Josef Raab. "Introduction: Interculturalism and Difference." In *Interculturalism in North America: Canada, the United States, Mexico, and beyond.* Eds. Josef Raab and Alexander Greiffenstern (Trier: Wissenschatlicher Verlag Trier & Tempe: Bilingual P, 2013), 1–26.
Hallowell, A. Irving. "Papers in Honor of Melville J. Herskovits: American Indians, White and Black: The Phenomenon of Transculturalization." *Current Anthropology* 4.5 (1963): 519–531.
Hollan, Douglas. "The Relevance of Person-centered Ethnography to Cross-Cultural Psychiatry." *Transcultural Psychiatry* 34.2 (1997): 219–234.
Kanter, Deborah E. "Their Hair Was Curly: Afro-Mexicans in Indian Villages, Central Mexico, 1700–1820." In *Crossing Waters, Crossing Worlds: The African Diaspora in Indian Country.* Eds. Sharon P. Holland and Tiya Miles (Durham, NC: Duke UP, 2006), 165–180.
McDonald, Dedra S. "Intimacy and Empire: Indian-African Interactions in Spanish Colonial New Mexico, 1500–1800." In *Confounding the Color Line: The Indian-Black Experience in North America.* Ed. James F. Brooks (Lincoln: U of Nebraska P, 1998), 21–46.
McFarren, Peter. "Afro-Bolivians Revitalize Their Cultural Identity." In *IndiVisible: African-Native American Lives in the Americas.* Ed. Gabrielle Tayac (Washington, DC: Smithsonian Books, 2009), 197–200.
Morner, Magnus. *Race Mixture in the History of Latin America.* Boston, MA: Little, Brown, and Company, 1969.
Palacio, Joseph. "The Sojourn Toward Self Discovery Among Caribbean Indigenous Peoples." *Caribbean Quarterly* 38.2–3 (1992): 55–72.
Palacio, Sr., Joseph O. "History and Continuity: Being Garifuna and Black Indian in the United States." In *IndiVisible: African-Native American Lives in the Americas.* Ed. Gabrielle Tayac (Washington, DC: Smithsonian Books, 2009), 91–98.
Sapir, Edward. "The Unconscious Patterning of Behavior in Society." In *The Unconscious: A Symposium.* Ed. E.S. Drummer (New York: Knopf, 1929), 114–142.
Shaler, N.S. "The African Element in America." *The Arena (Boston, Mass.)* 2 (1890): 660–673.
Smithsonian. "IndiVisible: African-Native American Lives in the Americas." http://www.nmai.si.edu/exhibitions/indivisible/making_connections.html. Accessed July 1, 2017.
Tannenbaum, Frank. 1992. *Slave and Citizen.* Boston, MA: Beacon Press.
Tayac, Gabrielle, ed. *IndiVisible: African-Native American Lives in the Americas.* Washington, DC: Smithsonian Books, 2009.
Thornton, Russell and Peter M. Nardi. "The Dynamics of Role Acquisition." *The American Journal of Sociology* 80.4 (1975): 870–885.
Zapf, Harald. "The Theoretical Discourse of Hybridity and the Postcolonial Time-Space of the Americas." *Zeitschrift für Anglistik und Amerikanistik* 47.4 (1999): 302–310.

7
A FINAL NOTE

Robert Keith Collins

The goal of this small edited volume is to revitalize interest in – and expand on – the study of African-Native Americans. The authors that have contributed to its contents and the lives that inform their research constitute present problems, perspectives, and prospects for further exploration of the relevance that African-Native American experiences hold for understanding the results of African and Native American contacts. African-Native Americans are part of history and a byproduct of African and Native American contacts that have occurred and continue into the present. As of Census 2010, there were 182,494 in the U.S. that identify as African American and Native American/Alaska Native and 112,207 that identify as African, Native American/Alaska Native, and White (Census.gov "The American Indian and Alaska Native Population: 2010" https://www.census.gov/history/pdf/c2010br-10.pdf. Accessed June 1, 2022; INEI. https://www.inei.gob.pe/media/MenuRecursivo/publicaciones_digitales/Est/Lib1642/cap03_03.pdf. Accessed June 1, 2022).

According to the census in Mexico, the first census to account for individuals of African descent, there are approximately 2.5 million people that identify as Afro-Mexican or of African descent. Given the Mestizo and Indigenous majority that constitute the population, a revisit of the Native American ancestry that Afro-Mexico embodies would further understandings of the unique aspects of African and Native American contact that this population represents within the Western Hemisphere (INEGI. "Demography and Society: Population." http://en.www.inegi.org.mx/temas/estructura/. Accessed June 1, 2022).

Peru's last official record of the Afro-Peruvian population occurred in 1940, with the question of race being removed by the next census; however, the question was added back in 2017 and approximately 828,800 identified as Afro-Peruvian or of African descent (afrodescendiente) (INEI. https://www.inei.gob.

DOI: 10.4324/9780429456459-11

pe/media/MenuRecursivo/publicaciones_digitales/Est/Lib1642/cap03_03.pdf. Accessed June 1, 2022). Laurence Foster (1978) reminded us in 1935 that,

> Throughout Latin America the extent of the interrelationships, both physical and cultural, between Indian and Negro has been very wide, much wider than the United States. But in both of the Americas a third factor… must be added to the relations between these two races, namely; the mixture of the whites with both of them.
>
> *(Foster 1978: 11)*

Foster's "third factor" that was later examined by sociologist Brewton Berry (1945) in "The Mestizos of South Carolina" shed light on explanatory gaps and research prospects on the subject of rural "tri-racial" isolates or rural individuals of blended African, Native American, and European ancestry and the need for further research on the population (Berry 1945: 1–3).

Although there are many more examples in the Americas, these three alone should not only encourage greater academic attention to the subject, but also shed light on the many frontiers for new knowledge acquisition about the dynamics of African and Native American contact in the Western Hemisphere. It is our sincere hope that this volume encourages intellectual pursuits that contribute to, and expand on, the literature on African-Native Americans (Collins 2006, 2009, 2021b, 91–92; Foster 1935: 9; Thornton 1998: 30; Woodson 1920: 45).

Toward a Twenty-First Century Study of African-Native Americans

To study African-Native Americans in the twenty-fist century is to not only expand on an empirically sound body of knowledge on African and Native American contact but to engage the relevance the research holds for descendants of these interactions in the present. If Africans and Native Americans had no contact, then there would be no individuals in W.P.A. slave narratives claiming Native American parentage and descent. There would be no stories of shared experiences as fellow slaves, shared resistance to racism, or treaties, particularly in 1866, requiring the recognition of former slaves as citizens by former slave-holding Native American nations (Collins 2017, 2020: 16–17; Porter 1932: 294; Sturm 2002: 1–5).

Native American nations, especially those in states with a legacy of Jim Crow laws, would not have to formulate tribal membership based upon blood quantum and, for some, in a way where Black blood becomes the criterion and boundary for who can be recognized as a tribal citizen and who cannot. There would also not be Native American mothers and fathers within African American families raising children with the tools to live as African American in U.S. society and at the same time with competence in tribal-specific cultural and linguistic practices. In a similar vein, there would be no Garifuna, Afro-Aymara, or Afro-Quechua and throughout the Western Hemisphere, there would have been no need for terms such as Mustee or Sambo or Negro being used as the only term to recognize children and cultural affiliates of African and Native American descent (Forbes 1983: 57–58; 1992: 1–5). There would also be no tribal citizens of African descent, many identifying tribal specifically, and embodying the inclusiveness and openness characteristic of many Native American societies before Jim Crow and blood quantum. Nor would these individuals be recognized by scholars as an under-research component of Native American population survival. The study of African-Native Americans could then be assumed esoteric and of potential importance to no one and Native American ancestry among African Americans a mere myth (Collins 2009: 183–184; Forbes 1992: 1–10).

Before the critical conversations generated by Dr. Tiya Mile's symposium "Eating Out of the Same Pot" that led to the interdisciplinary edited volume, "Crossing Waters Crossing World: The African Diaspora in Indian Country," scholars in the fields of anthropology, particularly what became Black Anthropology, history, sociology, and later Native American Studies, dedicated their careers to the study of this "third" avenue of contact that complemented studies preceding or occurring in tandem with those on European contact with Native Americans and Native American contact with Europeans. In light of the building of this complex body of literature, one may ask, as I am often, why African-Native Americans have not been part of common knowledge, especially in the U.S. The answer is quite complex and context dependent (Hallowell 1963: 519–525).

In some cities and towns along the Eastern Seaboard and in parts of the Southeastern U.S., including mid-Western States like Arkansas, Oklahoma, and Texas, some African-Native Americans, particularly tribal citizens, have a long tradition of being recognized socially and their understandings of selves are occasionally discussed as part of the Black population within communities, while others are not. For example, In 1935 Foster (1978) reminded us, in his observations and analyses of African Seminole lived experiences in Brackettville, Texas, and Nacimiento, Coahuila, Mexico, this is largely due to the "race complex" and racism that individuals choose to practice.

> With determined propaganda, certain whites in the United States have worked persistently to change the attitude of the Indians of the United States from friendly lines to positive opposition to the Negro. The amount of opposition which the Negro meets from the Indian in any given locality varies directly with the strength and persistency of the race complex in that locality.
>
> *(Foster 1978: 75)*

The same could be said of legal recognition. As lingering controversies over the Freedmen of the Cherokee, Chickasaw, Choctaw, Creek, and Seminole

Nations have shown, legal recognition remains a source of great contention and community and family divisions where Black blood is concerned, especially if a state charter grants Native Americans the status of White people and uses a one-drop rule definition for anyone of African descent (Sturm 2002: 1–3). In Mexico, Central, and South America, some Afro-Indigenous populations within and outside of indigenous communities are recognized, such as the Black Carib, Garifuna, Meskito, Afro-Aymara, and Afro-Quechua, etc., while others are not and accept being recognized as Mestizo or Negro, or embrace both, while maintaining Indigenous cultural and/or linguistic practices (Collins 2009, 2017, 2021b; Tayac 2009). These incredible cultural variations and inconsistencies in identification and recognition patterns remain in need of intellectual discourse on the histories and current efforts at self-determination asserted by these dynamic populations.

As has been discussed in this volume, the study of African-Native Americans has received significant anthropological attention since 1891. Given the numerous explorer and clergy reports from the historical record that informed Chamberlain's research, the date for actual documentation of the phenomenon can be said to be much older. The Civil Right movements of the 1960s brought attention to the respective and shared experiences with ongoing discrimination and institutionalized racism faced by African Americans and Native Americans. The Student Strike at San Francisco State University in 1968 that followed raises awareness to the fact that discrimination and racism were social phenomena that permeated higher education and the need for culturally relevant instruction in college classrooms. While African American Civil Rights were central in the push for culturally relevant education, unified efforts with Native Americans, as well as Asian Americans and Latinos, broadened the scope of needed attention on social justice for not just people of color, but the hundreds of White American supporters and first-generation college students themselves. Together, these efforts contributed to and enabled the formation of Ethnic Studies and the broader and comparative perspectives that characterize the various disciplines today. In a similar vein, out of these efforts Native American Studies was created at SF State and U.C. Berkeley (Sacks 1989: 534–535).

The following year, Native American movement organizer and scholar Jack D. Forbes joined the faculty of the University of California at Davis. His courses and research furthered the exploration of the intersections between African American and Native American histories and historical identities, as well as African American and Latin American histories, with particular attention to indigenous histories. Such courses were also part of the curriculum of Deganawida – Quetzalcoatl University (DQ), which he helped to co-found.

This pedagogical knowledge was followed by a course on Black Indians at San Francisco State University and the University of California (U.C.) at Berkeley. Courses at U.C. Berkeley focused on the experiences and identities of African-Native American populations within the U.S. At the beginning of the twenty-first century and in tandem with the groundbreaking exhibit

"IndiVisible: African-Native American Lives in the Americas," the American Indian Studies Department at San Francisco State redesigned its course to provide a hemispheric approach to the topic. Although questions continue about the importance of this area of study, the student response has been great curiosity. Students, especially White American students, seem intrigued by the resilience of African descended individuals in the face of cultural change, the breadth, scope, and frequency of African and Native American contacts, the existence of anti-Black racism in Native America, as well as the breadth and depth of Native American cultural impacts on African cultural change through association as slave holders, fellow slaves, and allies in resistance. It is also a chance for all students to see that slavery and racism were both Southern institutions and American institutions (Johnson and Smith 1999: 1–2).ssss

Some of these very students have gone on to Ph.D. programs in anthropology, history, sociology, while others pursue an M.A. in Ethnic Studies or Native American Studies. What they all share in common is a desire to contribute by uncovering new histories and individual lived experiences that reflect these contacts. For many African American students and Native American students with African American ancestry, it is a chance to explore the myths and truths, nature and sources, behind claims of Native American ancestry. For those students of more recent African and Native American parentage, it is a chance to experience relevant education and see that they are part of a much larger history of contact between these resilient populations in the Western Hemisphere. Studying African-Native Americans, making the histories part of the curriculum through course and textbook adoptions, and cultivating and supporting academic revitalization of areas of interest on this phenomenon offers great prospects for understanding the African diaspora among Native Americans beyond and/or in tandem with discourse on European expansionism (Hallowell 1955: 1–3, 1963: 519–520).

Where Do We Go from Here?

A.F. Chamberlain's paper in 1891 was not merely a presentation of cultural and historical events on contact between Africans and Native Americans, but a roadmap for finding academic and scientific explanatory gaps that future scholars could follow. According to Chamberlain (1891),

> To make the study of the contact of the African and the American as complete as possible, it is highly desirable that attention should be paid to the obtaining of information regarding (1) the results of the intermarriage of Indian and negro, the physiology of the offspring of such unions; (2) the social status of the negro among the various Indian tribes, the Indian as a slave-holder, the opinion the negro has of the Indian; (3) the influence of the Indian upon the negro, and of the negro upon the Indian, mythology and folklore.
>
> *(Chamberlain 1891: 90)*

Current research, including the works within these pages, also allude to the importance of adding to this list continued investigation of the similarities and differences in opinions held by Native Americans from federally recognized nations vs. non-federally recognized nations toward African Americans. These types of investigations allow for progress to be made and lend to greater understanding of African-Native American being and belonging (Tayac 2009: 19).

As contributing scholars have demonstrated, the study of African-Native Americans can be developed further in the fields of African American Studies, American Indian/Native American Studies, anthropology, history, and sociology. Works by non-academic scholars can also enhance knowledge of the phenomenon and its salience in identities today. During the symposium that preceded the opening of "IndiVisible: African-Native American Lives in the Americas" in 2009, co-curators, scholars, and community members acknowledged the importance of candidly examining the similarities and differences between African American and Native American attitudes toward one another, how they have changed over time, and shaped the lived experiences of African-Native Americans. It is also important to further problematize African-Native American understandings of being and belonging and why some African-Native Americans identify with being Native American descendants and tribal citizens, while others do not. In the absence of a new symposium, this edited volume fills a gap by showing the linkage between old and new perspectives on African-Native Americans (Littlefield 1978: 1–5, 1979: 1–10).

Interdisciplinary collaboration on the subject of African-Native Americans has occurred for quite some time, and this edited volume expands on that tradition by illuminating the different ways African-Native Americans have and can be researched. Given the growing diversity of the African-Native American population in the U.S., research in Mexico, Central, and South America, as well as among African-Native American immigrant populations, like some Garifuna, can inform us of how being African-Native American, beyond blood quantum, as it may not exist in their countries of origin, has and continues to change our societal definitions and expectations of who is African American and who is Native American (Collins 2009: 183–185; Davis 1991: 1–5; Johnson and Smith 1999: 1–10; Miles and Holland 2006: 1–5).

Another prospect for research is African-Native American population change and why some identify as African American, while others identify as Native American. Laurence Foster (1935) offered some great advice for furthering research in this area. Studies of this phenomenon will be difficult and complex. For the anthropologist, it will be important to remember that during analyses, it is likely that "…various types of data presented belong to widely different fields, and yet so long as they pertain to man, they are conceivably within the realm of anthropology" (Foster 1935: 76). For all scholars, however, the statistical analyses required to do the subject justice will need to remember that, "Indeed, statistics are valuable but there are many items which tend to complete the life, action, and thinking of a tribe which cannot be statistically expressed"

(Foster 1935: 76) and the voices of the people, especially on the consistencies and inconsistencies of identification and recognition, will need to complement statistical data. Unfortunately, such research may also reveal inconsistencies between current politics and racial expectations. Further research will not only require a thorough examination of census data, but also ethnographic field work that examines the honesty and dishonesty behind the documentation and recognition in the historical record, or lack thereof, of the Native American ancestry of African descended individuals. Ultimately, further academic study of African-Native Americans will need to be done by students of culture, history, and/or science dedicated to the academic, ethnographic, political, and scientific importance of understanding African-Native Americans. Analyses of this nature hold the potential to further our understanding of how and why their experiences – past and present – were not myths, but evidence of gaps in documentation, evident in the anthropological and historical records, in need of renewed academic interest (Davis 1991: 1–5).

Works Cited

Berry, Brewton. 1945. "The Mestizos of South Carolina." *The American Journal of Sociology* 51, no. 1: 34–41.

Census.gov. 2010. The American Indian and Alaska Native Population: 2010: 2010 Census Briefs. https://www.census.gov/history/pdf/c2010br-10.pdf. Accessed June 1, 2022.

Chamberlain, Alexander Francis. 1891. "African and American: The Contact of Negro and Indian." *Science* 17, no. 419 (February 13): 85–90.

Collins, Robert Keith. 2006. "Katimih o Sa Chata Kiyou? (Why Am I Not Choctaw?): Race in the Lived Experiences of Two Black Choctaw Mixed Bloods." In *Crossing Waters, Crossing Worlds: The African Diaspora in Indian Country*, edited by Sharon P. Holland and Tiya Miles, 260–272. Durham, NC: Duke University Press.

———. 2009. "What Is a Black Indian? Misplaced Expectations and Lived Realities." In *IndiVisible: African-Native American Lives in the Americas*, edited by Gabriella Tayac. Washington, DC: Smithsonian Books, 183–196.

———. 2017. *African and Native American Contact in the U.S.: Anthropological and Historical Perspectives*. San Diego, CA: Cognella Press.

———. 2020. "How Africans Met Native Americans during Slavery." *Contexts*, 19, no. 3 (Summer 2020): 16–21.

———. 2021a. "How Did Black Folks Become Indians? What Lived Experiences Say about Belonging, Culture, and Racial Mixture in Native America." In *The Complexities of Race: Identity, Power, and Justice in an Evolving America*, edited by Charmaine Wijeyesinghe, 126–147. New York: NYU Press.

———. 2021b. "Toward an Inter-American Study of African Transculturalization in Native America." In *Colonialism, Coloniality, and Decolonization in the Americas*, edited by Josef Raab and Alexia Schemien, 91–102. Tempe, AZ: Wissenschaftlicher Verlag Trier/Bilingual Press.

Davis, F. James. 1991. *Who Is Black?: One Nation's Definition*. University Park: Pennsylvania State University Press.

Forbes, Jack D. 1983. "Mustees, Half-Breeds and Zambos in Anglo North America: Aspects of Black-Indian Relations." *American Indian Quarterly* 7, no. 1: 57–83.

———. 1984. "Mulattoes and People of Color in Anglo-North America: Implications for Black -Indian Relations." *Journal of Ethnic Studies* 12, no. 2: 17–61.

———. 1992. *Africans and Native Americans: The Language of Race and the Evolution of Red-Black Peoples.* 2nd ed. Urbana: University of Illinois Press.

Foster, Laurence. 1935. *Negro-Indian Relations in the Southeast.* New York: AMS Press.

Foster, Laurence. 1978. *Negro-Indian Relations in the Southeast.* New York: AMS Press.

Hallowell, A. Irving. 1955. *Culture and Experience.* Philadelphia: University of Pennsylvania Press.

———. 1963. "Papers in Honor of Melville J. Herskovits: American Indians, White and Black: The Phenomenon of Transculturalization." *Current Anthropology* 4, no. 5 (December): 519–531.

INEI. "Poblacion Afroperuana." https://www.inei.gob.pe/media/MenuRecursivo/publicaciones_digitales/Est/Lib1642/cap03_03.pdf. Accessed June 1, 2022.

INEGI. "Demography and Society: Population." http://en.www.inegi.org.mx/temas/estructura/. Accessed June 1, 2022.

Johnson, Charles, and Patricia Smith. 1999. *Africans in America: America's Journey through Slavery.* 1st Harvest ed. San Diego, CA: Harcourt Brace.

Littlefield, Daniel. 1978. *The Cherokee Freedmen: From Emancipation to American Citizenship.* Santa Barbara, CA: Greenwood Press, 1–5.

———. 1979. *Africans and Creeks: From the Colonial Period to the Civil War.* Santa Barbara, CA: Greenwood Press, 1–10.

Miles, Tiya, and Sharon Patricia, Holland. 2006. *Crossing Waters, Crossing Worlds: The African Diaspora in Indian Country.* Durham, NC: Duke University Press.

Porter, Kenneth W. 1932. "Association as Fellow Slaves." *Journal of Negro History* 17, no. 3 (July): 294–297.

Sacks, Karen Brodkin. 1989. "Toward a Unified Theory of Class, Race, and Gender." *American Ethnologist* 16, no. 3: 534–550.

Sturm, Circe. 2002. *Blood Politics: Race, Culture, and Identity in the Cherokee Nation of Oklahoma.* Berkeley: University of California Press.

Tayac, Gabrielle, ed. 2009. *IndiVisible: African-Native American Lives in the Americas* 1st ed. Washington, DC: Smithsonian Institution's National Museum of the American Indian in association with the National Museum of African American History and Culture and the Smithsonian Institution Traveling Exhibition Service.

Thornton, Russell, ed. 1998. *Studying Native America: Problems and Prospects.* Madison: University of Wisconsin Press.

Woodson, Carter G. 1920. "The Relations of Negroes and Indians in Massachusetts." *Journal of Negro History* 5, no. (January): 45–57.

INDEX

activism 31, 34, 35, 39
African-American (s) 2, 18, 23, 45, 57, 58, 60, 61, 65, 70–74, 76, 101, 107–108, 112–117
African-Native 23, 24, 70, 72, 74, 77
Afro-Bolivian 106–107
Afro-Indigenous 28, 31–32, 37, 49, 115
Afro-Latin 107–109
Afro-Mexican 105
Afro-Peruvian 112
Afro-Taino 106
amalgamation 13, 70, 84
Anishinaabe 30, 38
anthropology 47, 51, 101, 103, 111, 114, 116
anti-Blackness 38
anti-miscegenation 41, 45
Aymara 105, 106–107, 114–115

being 49, 58, 63, 73, 83, 86
belonging 7, 14–15, 29–31, 43, 66, 69, 71
Black-Indian 6, 14, 22, 57, 59, 61–62, 70, 73, 75, 77
Black-Native 3, 5, 27–28, 38, 58
Blackness 72, 83
blood 43–48, 50, 58, 60, 69, 71, 73
blood quantum 5, 16, 22, 46–48, 58, 69, 71, 113, 117

Caribbean 19, 30, 59, 63, 83, 101–102, 108
Catawba 59, 64
census 3, 31, 41, 46, 49, 50, 60, 69, 71, 112, 118
Chamberlain, Alexander Francis 2, 13, 23, 116

Cherokee 18, 29, 48, 58, 61, 65, 68–69, 74
Chicago, Il 32, 74, 107
Chickasaw 9, 114
Chippewa 72
Choctaw 18, 61, 65, 114
citizenship 27–29, 33
class 27, 32
classification 5, 21–22
colonialism 19, 27–29, 31, 33–37
community 4, 61, 71, 85, 90–94, 105, 107–108, 115, 117
Creole 30–31
culture xii, 5, 17–18, 38, 58–60, 69, 71, 73, 74, 76–77, 83–86, 88, 91, 93–95, 104–109, 118

decolonization 36
demography 112
Detroit, MI 5, 27–36, 72
dispossession 27, 30, 43

embody 2, 5, 8, 107–110, 114
enslavement 8, 36–38, 61–64, 101
ethnographic 103–105, 109, 118
eugenics 41–50
Euro-American 1, 17, 62, 64
extermination 34

family 5, 14, 35, 45, 48
Forbes, Jack 59, 63, 115

Garifuna 102, 105, 107–109, 115
genealogy 37, 45
Gullah 76
Guyana 31

history 109, 112, 116
hypodescent 43, 58

identity 34, 41–44, 46, 48, 57, 62, 70, 72
Indianness 42, 48, 50, 58, 69, 71–73
indigenous 7, 27–31
IndiVisible 3, 22–23, 77, 105, 107, 117
Inter-American xi, 7
intermarriage xii, 3, 8, 13, 14, 42, 46, 49, 63, 91, 93, 101, 116

Katz, William Loren 6, 13, 14, 57, 60
kinship xii, 1–2, 5, 14–18, 23, 64, 93, 103, 105, 109

Lumbee 48

marginalized 3, 18, 58, 83
Mashantucket 85, 95
Massachusetts 85, 95
Memoirs 70
Mexico 1, 8, 16, 19, 21, 59, 61, 101–105, 107, 109, 112, 114–115
Michigan 8, 37, 72, 77
miscegenation 50, 101
Mississippi 47, 64
mixed-blood 15, 72
mixed-race 60, 62, 64, 69, 70, 72
Mohegan 85, 92, 94
Mulatto 19, 21, 104
multiracial 58, 60, 77
Mustee(s) 18–20, 22–23, 114

narrative(s) 3, 16–17, 33, 70–74
negro 2–5, 13, 15–16, 18–20, 23, 114–116
Negro-Indian 5–6, 59
Nicaragua 102, 107

Oklahoma 16, 28, 59, 65–69, 74–75, 114

Pequot 18, 21, 70, 86–87, 89, 92
Peru 104, 112
Pow-Wow 8, 83, 86

race xii, 2–3, 7–8, 13, 18, 22–23, 27–29, 43, 46, 49–50, 58–64, 66, 69–70, 72, 75–77, 85, 94
radicals 28–29, 31, 36
recognition 5, 7, 86, 104–105, 113–115, 118
removal 41, 42, 64–65, 67–68

self-determination 72
Seminole 6, 64, 75–76, 114
Shinnecock 85, 92, 94
slavery xii, 6, 15, 17–18, 20–21, 23, 28, 43, 59–61, 63–64, 67–68, 75, 89, 102–103, 107, 116
sovereignty 6, 17, 64, 72, 74–75
sterilization 45

Venezuela 21, 102, 108
Virginia 20, 42–43, 45, 46, 48–50

Wampanoag 18, 88–89
Woodson, Carter G. 3–4

Printed in the United States
by Baker & Taylor Publisher Services